ALAMO
— OF THE —
REVOLUTION

Benedict Arnold and the
Massacre at Fort Griswold

Jerald P. Hurwitz

A KNOX PRESS BOOK
An Imprint of Permuted Press
ISBN: 978-1-68261-953-7
ISBN (eBook): 978-1-68261-954-4

Alamo of the Revolution:
Benedict Arnold and the Massacre at Fort Griswold
© 2020 by Jerald P. Hurwitz
All Rights Reserved

Permuted Press, LLC
New York • Nashville
permutedpress.com

Published in the United States of America

1 2 3 4 5 6 7 8 9 10

This book is dedicated to my father, Payson Hurwitz, a World War II veteran and inspiration for this book, and to my wife, Rachelle, and my children, Asher and Felicia, for their love and support through some very dark days when my ability to write this book was very much in doubt.

Table of Contents

Preface

M ost Americans today are familiar with the story of the Alamo, and how in 1836 in the Texas War of Independence, some 180 Texan patriots, after refusing to surrender, died defending a makeshift fort against overwhelming numbers of Mexican regulars, led by the infamous General Santa Anna. Yet the vast majority of Americans have never heard of the defense of Fort Griswold, and the story of how some 162 American Revolutionary War patriots fought against a force of British regulars almost four times their number. Like the story of the Alamo, the author of the massacre was likewise infamous and ruthless. That leader was the notorious turncoat and fellow Nutmegger Benedict Arnold. Similar to the story of the Alamo, the American garrison was threatened with annihilation if they did not capitulate immediately. As at the Alamo, the garrison refused to be intimidated by the threat of no quarter and put up a stubborn defense against overwhelming odds. As a consequence, the defenders were very nearly slaughtered to the last man, but unlike those defenders of the Alamo a half century later, some were spared and some escaped and thus survived to tell their story.

On September 6, 1781, six weeks before Cornwallis's surrender at Yorktown to Washington ended major combat operations in America's War of Independence, 162 American patriots,[1] composed of militia, state troops, sailors from American privateers, and ordinary citizen volunteers, defended a stone and earthen fort against the assault of 750 seasoned British regulars[2] commanded by their former neighbor, Benedict Arnold. General Arnold, in his new role as a British brigadier general, was leading a punitive expedition against Connecticut's largest seaport, New London. New London, named after the city of London in 1668, is located a few miles up from the mouth of the Thames River, the largest river east of the Connecticut River in the state. In 1781, New London was known to have one of best deep water harbors in America. It afforded shelter from storms in Long Island Sound, and the pirate Captain Kidd in the early 1700s reputedly took refuge there.[3]

Across the Thames River lies the town of Groton. There, atop a glacial moraine that towers 120 feet above the river, the state of Connecticut constructed Fort Griswold to protect and defend New London's busy harbor. There, the bloodiest engagement ever fought in the state of Connecticut took place.

Very little has been written about this incident. It is largely ignored and unknown outside the southeast section of Connecticut. The most comprehensive study of the campaign was Walter Powell's book *Murder or Mayhem?* which is cited in the bibliography. It combined many of the firsthand accounts published in William Harris's 1882 book *The Battle of Groton Heights*, a compilation of firsthand and contemporary accounts and survivor family recollections with facts and figures regarding the importance of New London and Groton during the Revolution.

This is a story of undaunted courage by male family members of a few dozen families living within the proximity of greater Groton, individual volunteers from neighboring communities, crew members of the ships anchored in New London harbor, and the forty regulars of the garrison of Fort Griswold and escapees of Fort Trumbull. It is also the story of outsiders: two African Americans, one a slave named Lambo Latham[4] owned by the official commander of the garrison of Fort Griswold, Captain William Latham, and the other a freeman by the name of Jordan Freeman,[5] the orderly or batman of the commanding officer of all southeastern Connecticut, Colonel William Ledyard; and finally, an American Indian of the local Pequot tribe named Tom Wansac,[6] who I believe joined the defenders as a volunteer gunner from one of the crews of the privateers in the New London harbor. According to one source, there was purportedly another Native American, Ben Uncas of the Mohegan tribe, but his presence at the fort is not otherwise noted in the historic documentation of the fort.[7]

In sharp contrast with the bravery of the garrisons of Fort Griswold and Fort Trumbull were the far more numerous militia members from the environs of New London and neighboring communities, who ran from the British at sight or watched the British and loyalist depredations from a safe distance. If those standing and watching from a few hundred yards away would have joined the garrison at the fort, there would have most likely been a very different outcome.

In addition to the fatal flaws in the design of the fortifications defending the harbor, the lack of preparedness by the defenders contributed mightily to the disaster. In light of the Americans' knowledge of the multitude of British naval depredations up and down the Connecticut coast in 1777 and 1778, they should have known better. In the midst of untold wealth derived from the success of the privateering from ships using New London as their base, the inhabitants starved the forts' garrisons of the bare necessities of food, clothing, and even ammunition, and maintained skeleton companies to man their forts.

This is also the story of betrayal. Connecticut loyalists played a major role in the attack on New London. None more than turncoat Connecticut native Benedict Arnold, who grew up just a few miles from Groton on the upper reaches of the Thames River to the north of New London in Norwich. It was he, more than anyone else, who was the greatest proponent of the attack, as well the commander of the entire British expeditionary force. Information on the state of the defenses was passed on to British Lieutenant General Sir Henry Clinton in New York by many (sic) "friends to government"[8] living among their neighbors in southeastern Connecticut. Many Connecticut loyalists joined Arnold's loyalist regiment called the American Legion, which was just one of four loyalist units to participate in the expedition.

What happened should not have been a surprise. By 1781, the British had attacked virtually every port on the coast of Connecticut west of New London. Nevertheless, a certain amount of complacency set in after 1778. Still, with all their lack of preparedness, the patriots almost succeeded in their defense of Fort Griswold. Circumstances and chance would play a significant role in the end.

Although I shall tell the story of Benedict Arnold's raid on the ports of New London and Groton, the preponderance of my story will focus on the assault of Fort Griswold and its aftermath. We have a plethora of firsthand accounts of the fighting by the defending survivors and the families of those who perished. In sharp contrast, there are no known firsthand accounts by the British assailants—just Arnold's report to Clinton on the attack on the fort.

PREFACE

Besides Arnold's overview of the assault, we have British Ensign Alexander Gray's hand-drawn detailed map with notes on what occurred at every section of the fort. A copy of that map is included in this book We also have the engraved map of William Faden of London, Faden was the king's official engraver and geographer. Both maps are highly detailed and provide great insights into how the attack unfolded. The Faden map follows Gray's hand-drawn map but is more detailed and includes a picture of the fort's flag, as well as the location of the fort's guns and their relative size based on the length of the lines representing the cannon's barrels. There are, however, some major contradictions in the description of the action. Where they differ, I chose to follow Ensign Gray's hand-drawn map.

Another useful map is the hand-drawn map of New London and Groton by Captain Daniel Lyman of Benedict Arnold's loyalist American Legion Regiment and a Nutmegger from Pomfret to the north of New London. Lyman's map provides a detailed drawing of the landings, approaches, topography, streets, landmarks, water depths, and British troop movements. The map is particularly useful in identifying the location of each of the participating units in their approaches to New London and Fort Griswold. It corroborates many of the accounts by eyewitness Americans and Arnold himself and identifies more clearly where the events they described occurred. That map is included in this book and will be referred to as the Lyman Map.

The numerous accounts on the American side are often disjointed and focused on the experiences of the individual survivor based on his position within the fort, which is, unfortunately, not clearly identified in most instances. My analysis often involved a careful examination of the recorded stories of survivors and a correlation of those stories with Ensign Gray's map. This synthesis of the many American accounts required considerable effort and some conjecture, but the end result is a coherent, logical, and realistic unfolding of the story of the assault and its aftermath.

There are a lot of what-ifs. So here it is, a seminal moment in the story of the American Revolution, lost to us by its close proximity in time to the final major battle in the war, Yorktown.

Benedict Arnold

Connecticut was Brigadier General Benedict Arnold's native state and Norwich, just upriver from New London, was his childhood home. As the son of a prominent Norwich sea captain, Arnold was long familiar with New London. He often accompanied his father on his many cruises down the Thames River. He knew its docks; he knew its families. He learned to navigate the river's shoals along its mouth on Long Island Sound.

Life of children in the eighteenth century was perilous. Benedict and his five siblings all fell ill to the scourge of diphtheria or yellow fever. Only Arnold and his older sister survived. Arnold's father suffered severe financial losses from which he never fully recovered during the War of Jenkins' Ear. He turned to the bottle and subsequently drank himself to death and brought poverty and disgrace to young Benedict.

As a young teenager who lost his father, Benedict had to rely on the charity of a wealthy neighbor to provide for himself and his mother. Arnold was provided a trade apprenticeship but would have none of it. He left the area, but never left the state. Rather, Arnold made his way west to that other great seaport of Connecticut, New Haven. There, he built a success-ful smuggling business with his merchant vessels by circum-venting British mercantile restrictions. When the Revolution began, Arnold did not hesitate to throw his lot in with the patriot cause. He pushed for an aggressive campaign against British interests, and in the process made many enemies among his fellow patriots by reason of his inability to play the politics of the day. It was he who conceived and implemented the taking of Fort Ticonderoga and secured its guns for Wash-ington's siege of Boston. It was he who advocated its use as a base of operations for an invasion of Canada, which he saw as preempting a British assault from the north.

In an age of limited warfare, Arnold waged total war. When retreating from Canada by ship, he shot his horse lest he fall into the hands of the pursuing British. For a man with no mil-itary training, he was a natural leader with dead-on instincts. He was driven. He invaded Canada overland through Maine, an unheard-of feat, almost took Quebec by stealth, and built our first flotilla on Lake Champlain. In October of 1776, he used that scratch-built flotilla to engage in a naval battle with the British on Lake Champlain called the Battle of Valcour Island. While suffering a defeat at the hands of the superior British naval forces, he nonetheless succeeded in frustrating a British invasion from Canada in 1776.

In the following year Arnold was largely responsible for relieving Fort Stanwix from a British siege and for two American victories at the battles of First and Second Freeman's Farm, the latter of which resulted in a serious wound to Arnold. Arnold is given considerable credit by historians for the ultimate Ameri-can defeat and capture of General John Burgoyne and his army at Saratoga in October of 1777. Likely due to the enemies he made among powerful figures, such as Horatio Gates, Arnold received no contemporary credit for his contribution to the American victory. Arnold grew bitter and frustrated in his ongoing battles with Congress for compensation for his lost personal fortune spent arming and equipping his men for the 1775–1776 Canadian campaign, as well as the defense of northern New York, including the building of this nation's first flotilla to defend Fort Ticonderoga. Arnold was also aggrieved with Congress' failure to accord him the well-earned rank of major general. As a military commander in Philadelphia, he fought with the revolutionary state government in Pennsylvania, which was bent on retribution against those who remained in the city during the British occupation. When he turned coat in 1780, he did so with a zeal every bit equal to that with which he had embraced the Patriot Cause back in 1775, but this time its purpose was to strike at the very heart of the American rebellion.

1908 photo of Fort Griswold, Ledyard (CT) Historical Society. This photograph was probably taken from the Fort Griswold Monument located to the north of the fort. Note the position of the north gate entrance and the redan protecting it in the lower right hand corner of the photograph.

New London
and Its Defenses

The Continental Congress recognized the importance of New London—with its population of five thousand seven hundred—as the only major naval station between New York City and Newport, Rhode Island.[9] As such, in late 1775, Congress ordered the port fortified and dispatched an engineer to begin the process of planning the harbor's defenses. It took years to build the fortifications around the harbor under the unflagging leadership of Colonel William Ledyard.

Fort Griswold, named after Lieutenant Governor Matthew Griswold of Connecticut, was one of just three fortifications guarding the harbor of New London, but of the three, it was the most important. The fort lay directly across the river from the New London docks. It sat in the town of Groton, on the top of a ridge called Groton Heights. The ridge towered some 120 feet above the Thames River, and the fort lay on its southern promontory, some two hundred yards from the water's edge.

Griswold's guns dominated the river, three quarters of a mile wide from Groton Heights on the eastern shore to the harbor of New London on the western shore. No enemy ship could attack the harbor without taking a shellacking from the big guns of the fort and the river battery just below the fort.[10]

The fort was in the shape of a trapezoid, with the western or river side curtain wall bounded by two irregular-shaped bastions anchoring the north and south ends of that western wall. The curtain walls of the western, northern and southern sides were around forty yards long, not counting the bastions. The corners on the longer seventy-yard eastern or inland-facing curtain wall had no corner bastions, but it did have an arrow-shaped projection in the center. This projection allowed defenders to pour enfilading fire into the flanks of attackers approaching from the east to assault the northeast or southeast corners of the fort.[11]

Upon completion, the fort was surrounded on its north and east sides with a four-foot-deep and ten-foot-wide ditch called a fosse or dry moat, not unlike a medieval moat minus the water. The fosse served to break up an assault, making the attackers more vulnerable to enfilading fire from bastions, and raising the fort's walls to sixteen feet or taller. There was no need for a fosse or dry moat on the south side and the river side because those sides sported high enough walls using the natural lay of the land and slope of the ridge. The fort was largely earthen, but the sixteen-foot-high outer walls on all but the river side were reinforced by stone. Each wall on the land sides and the riverside bastions contained angled, wedge-shaped openings called embrasures, from which cannon could be placed to fire from a protected narrow opening on the inside of the wall. Each embrasure widened as it approached the outside of the wall. This served to maximize the field of fire from each cannon while at the same time protecting the cannon's crew from small arms fire and enfilading artillery fire. In between the embrasures, the inside earthen walls contained firing steps—also called—banquettes from which the defenders could step up to fire their muskets over the top of the wall (the parapet), and then step down to load behind the wall's protection. The walls and bastions facing the land approaches to the fort were fraised, which means they sported eighteenth-century obstacles in the form of twelve-foot-long, heavy, thick, round and sharpened wooden stakes planted in the fort's earthen wall horizontally or tilted obliquely at a downward or upward angle so that they protruded between six and eight feet from the curtain wall. The fraise was used in a similar fashion and for a similar purpose as barbed wire in modern warfare to impede and slow attackers' approach.[12] The wooden stakes were placed close enough to each other that a man could not squeeze his body between them. These sharpened stakes slowed the attackers and canalized or diverted their approach. Fraises forced attackers to work upside down to extract the stakes or to climb out and over them, which slowed down attackers and rendered them more vulnerable to defenders' gunfire and grenades.

A wooden platform or floor supported the weight of each cannon at each firing position on the ramparts. The platform allowed the guns to recoil backward smoothly, allowing ready access to the gun's muzzle for reloading, and prevented the cannon from sinking into the underlying earthen floor. All cannon were loaded from the muzzle, not from the breach, in contrast to modern cannon.

On the river side or western wall, there were no embrasures, except on the river side section of the northwest bastion. The guns were said to be placed *en barbette* or over the parapet next to each other without the protection afforded by the sides of embrasure walls as to projectiles fired at the cannon or crew from any angle other than head on. In contrast to the cannon placed "en barbette", most of the cannon in the fort were placed at the angled openings in the curtain wall called "embrasures". Embrasures while providing a modicum of protection to the gun crew and cannon restricted the cannon's field of fire. The cannon on the western curtain wall of the fort were placed en barbette to maximize the number of cannon that could be placed on the river side wall and expand their field of fire. No allowance was to be made for use of that section of the fort for small arms fire. This made sense because the primary purpose of the river side guns was to engage enemy ships coming up the river. Because range was a greater factor here than the ability of the cannon to serve as an antipersonnel weapon, the heaviest guns of the fort, mostly 12-pounder cannon (a large cannon for its day, as the size of its barrel allowed it to fire 12-pound iron balls), would have been placed there to inflict maximum damage on wooden hulled vessels and their rigging as they made their way to the harbor, almost a mile away from the fort's guns. They would later be called a barbette battery to differentiate them from the guns positioned at the embrasures. Undoubtedly, most (if not all) of such river-facing cannon barrels were mounted on four-wheel truck garrison carriages (a carriage borne by four small, solid wheels independently attached to the carriage cheeks and often made of iron for stability on a flat surface). In contrast to field cannon carriages, the wheels were not attached to an axel. Field cannon carriages sported two large, wooden spoke-filled carriage wheels mounted on an iron axel and a two-pronged trail intended for stability; these carriages increased mobility over uneven surfaces, such as rocky terrain.[13]

The fort's double gate of heavy wood was located in the middle of the north wall. It was guarded by a ravelin, an open-backed, arrow-shaped earthen outer work with two faces, whose main purpose was to prevent an attacker from firing cannon directly at the gate. Because it was open to the back, it was not intended to be manned, but merely to prevent the enemy from firing directly at the gate. In some forts, where the ravelin was manned, it was completely enclosed and connected by a movable raised bridge to the fort's rampart (as at the eighteenth century Fort Stanwix in Rome, New York), but not here.[14]

On the south side of the fort was an entrance called a sally port. It was designed to permit the defenders to sortie out of the fort to launch a preemptive strike on an attacker. To avoid serving as a conduit into the fort for an attacker, the sally port was built as a narrow tunnel through the fort's south wall, wide enough for just one person to pass at a time. It zigged and zagged in a way that gave every advantage to a right-handed defender. This fort's sally port emptied out to a protected passageway or trench that led down the hill to the water battery, which was composed of 18-pounders close to the river.

Inside the fort, there was a capacious barracks building supposedly capable of housing three hundred men that sat on the parade along the eastern side of the fort (the open ground on the interior of a fort is called the parade). In the northwest corner of the fort's parade was the well, the only source of water in the fort.[15]

Placed under the southwest bastion was the fort's powder magazine, containing hundreds of pounds of black gunpowder in barrels, as well as artillery projectiles and musket cartridges. The southwest bastion was where the fort's flagstaff stood. The flag flown was probably thirteen red-and-white stripes as evidenced by the lines on Faden's flag representation in his engraved map of the fort. That bastion also contained the most vulnerable part of the fort. The fort's builders incorporated a large, twelve-foot-high granite outcropping, a vestige of the glacier that scoured out the river valley in the last ice age, as part of the wall rather than removing it. That large rock prevented fraising, and because it was largely set at right angles to the ground rather than sloping, would shield an attacker below the wall from defending musket fire.[16]

Many eighteenth-century forts were picketed on the outside or inner part of the ditch, but that does not appear to be the case with Fort Griswold. Picketing refers to placing sharpened wooden poles vertically inside or outside the fosse. For an example of such pickets in a ditch or fosse, see Don Troiani's painting of the final British assault on the southern curtain wall on the cover of this book.[17]

It was also common to have the fields around the fort cleared of trees and buildings and covered by abatis, another form of eighteenth-century obstacle akin in purpose to barbed wire in the twentieth century. Abatis consisted of uprooted trees placed next to each other with their branches directed toward the attacking enemy. It was designed to slow down an attacker by entangling his troops in the branches and roots of the closely placed uprooted trees. Abatis were devastatingly effective against the British assault at Fort Ticonderoga in 1758 during the French and Indian War, and against the Hessians at Fort Mercer in 1777, but there is no mention of them in the battle reports, or in the known soldiers' and participants' memoirs. There was supposed to be abatis around the fort according to correspondence dated a few years earlier,[18] but it must have been so degraded by age and full of enough gaps to not constitute any great impediment to the attackers. Whatever the reason, no mention was made of it in the known accounts of the battle.

There was yet one more element to the defense at Fort Griswold. About 120 yards to the east of the fort was a flèche (an open-backed, arrowhead-shaped earthwork with three small cannon (iron 4-pounders) intended to cover a hidden eastern land approach to the fort.

Across the river on the western shore of a rocky outcrop extending into the river just below the docks of New London sat Fort Trumbull, named for Connecticut's wartime governor Jonathan Trumbull. It was really just a water battery with no rear fortifications to guard it from a land assault.

Fort Town Hill, the third fortification protecting New London harbor, was a small earthen-and-stockade affair located on a modest hilltop in the western part of New London. It was supposed to protect the land approach to Fort Trumbull. It was not taken seriously as a fortification by anyone, as might be surmised by its nicknames: Fort Nonsense by the Americans and Fort Folly by the British.

Heavy cannon taken from Commodore Hopkins's 1776 raid on the Bahamas's Fort Nassau would gird the harbor's forts and water batteries. Although all the forts sported cannon (Fort Griswold alone had twenty-three) with another ten below on the Groton water battery, the state of Connecticut afforded a mere two companies of twenty-five men each to man the guns of these three fortifications. Congress had authorized three artillery companies for the planned three fortifications back in 1777. The Connecticut General Assembly soon after resolved that the three artillery companies be composed of fifty-four men each. A year later, the assembly reduced the authorized companies to two, an inadequate number, but the poor, uncertain pay and inadequate supplies contrasted with the easy and large sums available to men willing to sign on with the many privateers running out of New London made even that lower number unattainable. In fact, the New London and Groton garrisons were literally starving in the midst of plenty. Colonel William Ledyard, commander of the New London and Groton defenses, had to furlough much of the garrison in the winter of 1780–1781 so they might feed and clothe themselves. Moreover, the shortage of gunpowder made it difficult for the companies to train and practice on the guns.[19]

One artillery company was assigned to Fort Trumbull, and the other to Fort Griswold. Given that the bare minimum required to man each cannon was four, the number of soldiers would have to be supplemented by unsteady and untrained militia. Even if the militiamen were accomplished in the use of their muskets, they were usually woefully unprepared to man the cannon.

Opposite: Faden Map of Fort Griswold, 1781. William Faden (1749–1836) was an English cartographer and a publisher of maps.

1. Magazine
2. Sally Port
3. A ditch leading to the battery below.
4. Emberizine (sic.) where Maj. Montgomery fell.
5. Barracks
6. Well
7, 8, 9. Points where the Light Company, Grenadiers, and the 40th Reg. of Foot entered.

10. Guns that much annoyed the troops.
11. Ravelin (sic.) that covered the gate.
F. A rock not cut away which gives an entrance into the work.

From E to F around the sides D, C & B the works are fraised on the curtain. A to the angle F it forms a barbette battery.

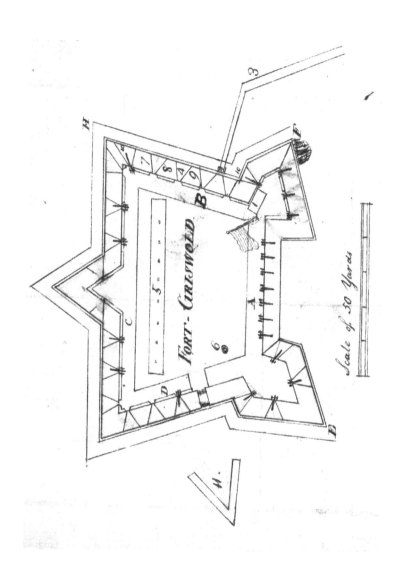

Interior view of the fort looking toward the flag pole on the SW Bastion with the sally port to the left and the magazine door in the center.

The British Decision to Attack New London

This nest of privateers at New London, a town with a population of close to six thousand inhabitants, a considerable number in eighteenth-century America, was located in the midst of two major occupied British ports (Newport, Rhode Island to the east and New York City to the west). With the British having the largest navy in the world, in contrast to a virtually nonexistent Continental Navy, why did the British wait so long to attack New London? During the course of the war, Connecticut privateers seized some five hundred ships, with most of those captured ships being taken to New London. Beginning with Lord William Tryon's raid on Danbury, Connecticut in April of 1777, the British launched a series of devastating, amphibious raids on Connecticut coastal towns. Danbury was not even on the coast; it was over twenty-five miles inland from the British landing site in Westport. That invasion force, while successful in destroying a Continental Army supply depot, was bloodied by Connecticut

militia led by none other than Benedict Arnold. He was returning from his ill-fated Canadian invasion and the destruction in
the fall of 1776 of his built-from-scratch American flotilla at the
Battle of Valcour Island on Lake Champlain.

The Danbury raid was followed by a series of British attacks over the next two years that left the Connecticut
coastal towns of Norwalk, Stratford, Fairfield, and New Haven
in smoking ruins. Only Stamford warded off a British raid by
a quick concentration of militia. Those ports were consider-
ably less important than New London. Yet the British did not
come. Perhaps it was the distance from New York or the successful blockade of the Thames River. In August of 1780, a large
British fleet lay off the mouth of the Thames. To defend the
port of New London, more than three thousand patriot militia encamped in and around Fort Griswold for two weeks. Not
wanting to face so great a force, the British left without making
any attempt to assault the harbor.

A year later, a combination of factors would lead the British
to try again. Probably the most important factor was Benedict
Arnold's changing sides in 1780. Arnold was a zealous officer,
who constantly sought opportunities to wage an aggressive war
more suited to the Age of Napoleon than the Age of Reason.
He constantly harangued Britain's commander in chief in America, Lieutenant General Sir Henry Clinton, to lead expeditions
against his former countrymen. It was Arnold who recognized
the vulnerability of Virginia and led a successful invasion to take
Portsmouth, Virginia in December of 1780. After a few months
of leading an overwhelmingly successful expedition to Virginia,
Arnold was superseded by Major General William Phillips and
recalled to New York. Arnold might have felt humiliated. He
paved the way for success, only to see his baby snatched from his
arms, even if Phillips outranked him and brought two thousand

reinforcements. Even though Phillips soon died of disease, he was quickly replaced by Lord Charles Cornwallis, who brought with him the survivors of the pyrrhic victory over Nathanael Greene's southern continental army at Guilford Courthouse in March of 1781.

Returning to New York, Arnold chafed at the inactivity of Lieutenant General Clinton. He pushed and prodded for an expedition against New England, particularly New London. Who was better to command such an expedition but a native son of the New London area, and a seasoned sailor of the Thames River? Clinton demurred. He was fixated on the threat of an assault against New York by George Washington and his French allies. Then something happened to change Clinton's mind.

The privateers hailing from New London had long been successful in picking off British merchantmen on the eastern seaboard. The *General Putnam* launched in April 1778 from Nathaniel Shaw's shipyard in New London captured fourteen British vessels before being destroyed or captured at the ill-fated expedition to Penobscot, Maine in August of 1779. She was just one of ten Shaw-owned-and-operated privateers using New London as a base. Shaw was only one local merchant among many who ran privateers out of New London. As the wealthiest and most prominent merchant in New London, Shaw was named the state's marine agent and given the power to direct and coordinate the activities of all state privateers and their operations. Operating from his large stone mansion, he sent these privateers out to sow havoc along British shipping lanes.[20]

If that were not enough, raids were launched from New London against British bases across the sound in Long Island. An unsuccessful raid had been launched from New London on July 12, 1781 and an even larger raid was being planned for later. None of these acts alone spurred the British to take action against the offending port. Then, a little more than a couple of weeks later, everything changed.

On July 31, 1781, the privateers literally hit the mother lode when Captain Dudley Saltonstall of the Brigantine *Minerva* captured the *Hannah*. The *Hannah* was laden with a fabulous cargo consisting of gunpowder and West Indian luxuries worth some eighty thousand pounds (many millions of American dollars in today's money). What's more, many of those luxuries were intended for British officers in New York.

Captain Watson of London, the captain of the merchant vessel *Hannah*, made his way back to New York. There, he complained loudly about the cursed rebels in New London, where the *Hannah* had been taken, and where the prized luxuries in its hold awaited sale. This was the final straw. Clinton, who recently learned that the French fleet had landed troops in Virginia, listened to Arnold argue that perhaps such a large raid might make the rebels think twice about venturing far from New York and New England to join their allies in Virginia. Clinton had contemplated his own larger raid against Newport, Rhode Island, which the British had evacuated in 1779. New London was closer. What's more, it merited retribution. He authorized Arnold on September 2 to take some 1,732 troops and twenty-four vessels on a punitive expedition against New London.[21]

This is an example of an 18th century fortification showing fraise and ditch on earthen fortifications. *William L. Clements Library, University of Michigan.*

"Trench leading from the water battery up to the sally port on the South Wall. A protruding portion of the Southwest Bastion is to the left."

The Expedition

A rnold would take three veteran regiments of British regulars: the yellow-faced 38th, the green-faced 54th, and the illustrious heroes of the Battle of Germantown, the buff-faced 40th. (Facings refer to the color of the lapels, cuffs and collars on the soldiers' orange brick red or madder red uniform coats.) To this force, Clinton added four loyalist units, the formerly green-coated Lieutenant Colonel Beverley Robinson's Loyal Americans, Arnold's own American Legion, Lieutenant Colonel Joshua Upham's Refugees, also known as the Associated Loyalists from New Jersey, and the 3rd New Jersey Provincial Battalion, commanded by Lieutenant Colonel Abraham Van Buskirk and made up of Bergen County Dutch descendants in their blue-faced madder red uniforms, along with assorted loyalist volunteers. We don't know the uniforms worn by Upham's Refugees. Were I to speculate, I would guess that Upham's men would be uniformed like the rest of the loyalist New Jersey line, with madder red coats sporting blue facings. Arnold's regiment the American Legion supposedly sported madder red coats faced green, similar to that of the Maryland and Pennsylvania loyalist units. The Loyal American Regiment had buff facings.[22]

To screen the landings and the approach of the line troops to their target, Clinton sent along 120 bicorne-wearing Hessian Jägers clad in dark green coats with crimson facings and carrying short rifles and swords in lieu of bayonets. These men were hunters and game wardens from the forests of Germany, where rifles were prized for their accuracy in hunting game.

There were also three dark-blue-coated, red-faced Royal Artillery gun crews to man three cannon to accompany the expedition.

There was one other addition to the expedition that was highly unusual: the two flank companies of the 40th regiment. Each British regiment—with certain exceptions—had but a single battalion of ten companies, optimally with sixty men each. Eight of the companies were composed of regular soldiers distinguished by the ubiquitous cocked hat. Such soldiers were called "hat men." The cocked hat was formerly a full-fledged tricorne at the beginning of the century, but over the years, it was gradually morphing into a bicorne. It would arrive at that final destination in the 1790s. The companies of hat men were called battalion companies. The remaining two companies of the battalion were called flank companies. They consisted of the grenadiers' company and the light infantry company (often called light bobs). These were more highly trained men, distinguished in the case of the grenadiers by their greater height and their tall bearskin caps, and in the case of the light bobs, distinguished by their short cut-down coats, red waistcoats, black (in lieu of white or buff) straps and belts, and usually some variation of short leather helmet with feathers. The light bobs were generally younger, more agile men trained for irregular combat. The grenadiers, in contrast, were the biggest, tallest, and most powerful men in the regiment.

The elite grenadier and light infantry companies were called flank companies because when the entire battalion assembled in line, the grenadier company formed to the right of the line, with the light infantry company to the left. Nevertheless, as a rule, the flank companies did not serve with their parent regiment's battalion companies, but instead converged with other regiments' elite companies of light infantry and grenadiers to form shock battalions.

The battalion companies of the 40th had only recently returned from several years of service in the disease-ridden West Indies. Their ranks were seriously depleted. To bring up their numbers, the regiment's flank companies were added, and as many as seventy replacements destined for other regiments were diverted to swell the ranks of the 40th's hat companies. As a result, the 40th's numbers would swell to 325 men. There is no evidence that the flank companies of the other two British regiments were attached to their hat companies.[23]

Arnold departed Whitestone in what is now New York City on September 4. His task force would rendezvous near Huntington, Long Island before descending on New London in the wee hours of September 6. What Arnold could not foresee was how his intended surprise attack could be thwarted by the myriad of spies on both sides that operated freely through no man's land. Information leaked through Westchester County like a sieve. Moreover, in the days of sail, any ship borne attack was subject to the vicissitudes of the tides and the winds. Arnold relied on the information obtained by spies and other "friends of the government" to anticipate the obstacles he would have to overcome in seizing the port. On the American side, a spy named Captain David Gray, with close relations to Clinton, rode out from New

York City on September 4 to warn Colonel Ledyard of Arnold's impending attack. He would arrive at New London on the evening of September 5. It was not clear what Ledyard did next to prepare for the attack, but he would not have much time.[24]

At three o'clock in the morning, Arnold's fleet was spotted off the mouth of the Thames by Sergeant Rufus Avery from Fort Griswold. Avery immediately fired off one of the two alarm guns located in the southwestern part of the fort. Captain William Latham immediately followed that discharge by firing the second alarm gun from the northwest side of the fort. The two cannon shots were intended to call out the militia, or at least all those within hearing distance, usually at least ten miles out. A year earlier, some three thousand militia had shown up at the fort in response to a perceived threat that never materialized. Unfortunately, Arnold knew all about the signal. All he needed to do to thwart its effect was to fire another gun after the first two were fired. Two cannon fired in succession meant an attack was imminent, but three cannon fired in succession meant a prize was being brought into the harbor. Many patriots who heard the third cannon blast assumed a prize was being brought in and went back to bed. Ledyard would have to dispatch riders to neighboring towns and outlying farms to rouse the militia while he assembled and readied the garrisons of Forts Trumbull and Griswold.[25]

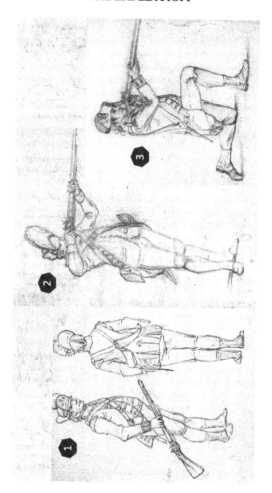

1. Light infantry. Short Coats, shoulder wings, caps, and in some cases, short rifles.

2. Grenadier firing. The bearskin, the sword, and the wings on the shoulders differentiate the member of the elite grenadier company from members of the battalion companies and light infantry.

3. Battalion soldier kneeling. Wearing a cocked hat, no sword, and no wings. Eighty percent of the regulars were "hat men."

Drawings by Philip James de Loutherburg, 1778 from the Anne S.K Brown Military Collection, courtesy of the John Hay Library at Brown University.

American Defense Preparations

L edyard began defense preparations in New London by sending gunpowder and food in barrels to the forts to sustain their defense. It would take time to assemble the militia and prepare the forts. Fate intervened and gave Ledyard the gift of time he so desperately needing. Arnold was immobilized off the coast, unable to unload his invasion force, due to the north wind and the outgoing tide. This providence would hold the British at bay for six hours.

After dispatching riders to the countryside to call out the militia and arranging for powder and food supplies to be sent to the fort, Ledyard went down to the harbor to the privateers to beseech the sea captains and their crews (estimated at over 220 men)[26] to volunteer their services to man the cannon at the forts. There were over fifty-eight cannon to staff, and only around fifty men to operate them.[27] Ledyard desperately needed men who knew how to load and fire cannon. He knew he could find such men among the crews of the many privateers in the harbor. What's more, such men were likely to be seasoned fighters. So Ledyard made his way down to the harbor and the ships. He was desperately hoping to persuade such men to forsake their vessels in the hopes of keeping the British at bay by manning the forts' guns.

When he arrived at the harbor, he found many of the captains and their crews frantically trying to save their ships by sailing up the river beyond the bar, toward the head waters of the Thames in Norwich. Like the British, the privateers were being thwarted by the north wind and outgoing tide. Ledyard had no power to compel them, so he had to settle on a handful of crews led by their captains.

One was Captain Peter Richards of the brig *Hancock*. Richards had served with John Paul Jones and had been captured by the British and imprisoned in Britain. He made a daring escape to France and returned to Connecticut to command his own privateer vessel named the *Hamilton*. Richards brought as many of his crew as he could, including one Christopher Latham. Latham's cousin, Elijah Latham, also went into Fort Griswold. Captain Elias Henry Halsey, probably with several of his crew, also left his privateer in the harbor to join the Griswold garrison, as did Captain Nathan Moore.[28]

There was confusion and panic in New London and Groton. Those who were able packed or hid their valuables and sent their families out of town. Others hunkered down to try to ride out the storm. Those with sick or disabled family members would have to rely on the not-so-tender mercies of the invaders. Even those so-called friends of the government scornfully known as Tories to the patriots could not be assured that their homes and valuables would be protected. Indeed, Arnold would torch their homes (in addition to those of their patriot neighbors) if just to shield them from retribution by their neighbors after his departure for having received favorable treatment.

Colonel William Ledyard sent his family away. Then, with his orderly, an African American named Jordan Freeman, he went down to the river to cross over to Groton. As he approached the river, he was accosted by anxious residents. He stood by the shore and assured the crowd as follows: "If I must lose honor or life today you, who know me best, can tell which it will be."[29] He then turned, boarded the boat, crossed the Thames, and ascended the hill to the fort.

There he was joined by his nephew Captain Youngs Ledyard of the militia. Other members of the militia came from Groton, as well as a sprinkling of men from neighboring New London and Stonington. Generally, it was a family affair, where all the men and boys of a family would come in together. For example, there were at least fifteen Averys, five Chesters, six Lathams, eight Perkinses, four Starrs, five Stantons, and five Williamses. Some were as young as Captain William Latham's twelve-year-old son Junior, and some as old as seventy-five-year-old John Comstock.

All morning, volunteers and militia dribbled in. Young volunteers like nineteen-year-old Benadem Allyn and his cousin Belton set out that morning on what they thought would be an exciting adventure. They stopped on their way to see Benadem's sister at the schoolhouse. In response to her inquiry about where they were going, Benadem responded, "Down to the training to see the fun."[30] His sister pleaded with them not to go, but they would not hear of it and continued on their way to the fort. Upon learning of Benadem's departure, his father grabbed his musket and mounted his horse in an effort to catch up with Benadem, but he was too late to join or stop his son.

Another group were the Chester brothers, Daniel, Charles, and Ensign Eldredge. Daniel had been a crew member of the Minerva. He joined his two brothers at the fort.[31] Twenty-one-year-old Samuel Edgecomb was big and powerful. He was plowing rye on his farm when he received word of the British invasion force. Like Cincinnatus, he left the oxen tethered to the plough and made for the fort, where he was joined by his brother Gilbert.[32]

Captain Hubbard Burrows, too, was at the plough when he was fetched by Edward Stanton and Thomas Williams from his militia company. Without unhitching his oxen, he ran to the house to grab his gun. He took his son with him so his son could take back his horse. As he was leaving, his wife yelled "When will you be back?" To which he replied: "Goodbye. God knows!"[33] He and Williams would never return and Stanton would be severely wounded.

An experienced officer, Captain Amos Stanton was home on leave from the Continental Army. He did not hesitate to volunteer his services to Colonel Ledyard. He was descended from an Indian warrior and from John Alden of the *Mayflower*. Four other Stantons were also in the fort. Lieutenant Enoch Stanton was second-in-command of Fort Griswold's garrison under Captain William Latham. His affianced widower brother, Sergeant Daniel Stanton, had been a member of the crew of the *Minerva* and had recently given his fiancé a brocade of silk for her wedding dress from his share in the spoils off the *Hannah*. He would have his two sons, Daniel Jr. and Edward, with him in the fort. Not one of them would be unscathed that day.[34]

Captain William Latham, the commander of the fort's garrison, had a slave named Lambert Latham, but called Lambo after the derogatory black name of Sambo. Before hurrying to Fort Griswold, the captain told his wife to pack their belongings in a farm wagon and to take his children, slaves (including Lambo), and servants with her to her uncle Parke Avery's homestead in the north of Groton. Upon arrival at the Avery homestead, Lambo took a musket that was in the wagon and returned south to join his master.[35]

One of the fort's garrison was Andrew Gallup. Andrew was a direct descendent of John Mason, the colonial leader of a bloody expedition during the Pequot War (1636–1637). In 1637, Mason's men surrounded a stockaded Pequot Indian village just a few miles east of Groton Heights, and after penetrating the stockade, Mason ordered his men to set fire to its wigwams, form a cordon around the village, and shoot all who attempted to flee the inferno. Many men, women, and children died in the blaze. Almost 150 years later, Andrew would be fighting side by side in the defense of the fort with a member of that tribe named Tom Wansac. As Tom was not known to be a member of the militia or the garrison, he was probably a member of one of the privateer crews that volunteered to man the cannon.[36]

Despite the ample time allowed by providence, the number of volunteers in Groton was little more than 110. When combined with the thirty or so men of the regular garrison, it was inadequate to cover the more than 220 yards of curtain wall, plus the yardage around the three bastions, let alone man the twenty-three cannon in the fort. Time was running out.

The boulder at the meeting of the two faces of the SW bastion from the defender's prospective on the parapet.

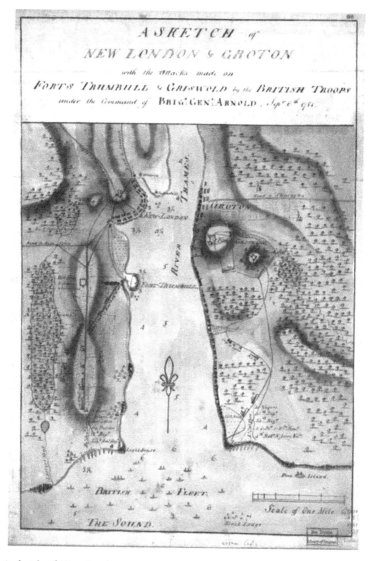

A sketch of New-London or Groton, with the attacks made on Forts Trumbull and Griswold by the British troops under the command of Brigr. General Arnold Sepr. 6th, 1781 / by Captain Lyman of ye Prince of Wales Amn. Volrs, *William L. Clements Library, University of Michigan.*

The West Shore Landing

About 9 AM, the wind changed and the British began to land their troops on both sides of the Thames. The process of disembarking 1732 men would take at least an hour. Arnold divided his force into two groups with roughly even numbers and led the force on the Thames' western bank, or the New London side. He took only one of three regiments of British regulars, the yellow-faced 38th regiment. The rest of his force was composed of three Loyalist regiments, the Loyal Americans (one of the older loyalist units), Upham's Refugees, and Arnold's own American Legion, along with about sixty Jägers and a company of the Royal Artillery with a 6-pounder cannon. The remaining units in the expedition, namely the 40th and 54th regiments, the 3rd New Jersey Provincial Battalion, and the remaining Jäger company and Royal Artillery crews were commanded by Lieutenant Colonel Edmund Eyre of the 54th Regiment of Foot. They were assigned to land on the east side of the Thames for the assault on Fort Griswold.[37]

We have two first-person patriot accounts of Arnold's west-bank assault. Forty-seven years after the attack, John Hempsted wrote of his role as a member of the 8th Connecticut militia regiment to meet the invading landing force. That morning, Hempsted climbed Prospect Hill about a half mile from his home and saw the invasion fleet lying off the coast. He returned home to have breakfast and to arrange to have his son take the wagon into town to evacuate his mother-in-law. Despite being in a northern state, it seems to have been quite common for middle-class families to own a young male slave to act as an errand boy. Hempsted reports that he retrieved his musket and cartridge box, then mounted his horse with his "little black boy" so he might ride to the militia's rendezvous site. He would rely on his "little back boy" to take his horse back home. As he was leaving, his wife called out to him that she had better not hear that he had been shot in the back.[38]

Hempsted rode out to Manwaring's Hill only to find no one there. He rode down the street to his deceased father's house, dismounted, and told his "boy" to take his horse back home while he made his way on foot to the beach. As he started out, he was met by two mounted officers, Captain Mallet and Captain John Deshon. They asked him to get on one of their horses and began riding toward the beach. On the way, they stopped at Lieutenant Colonel Joseph Harris Jr.'s home and asked for news and orders. Harris, the second-in-command of the 3rd Connecticut militia regiment on the New London side of the river, said the British were already landing on the beach and that they should all go down to Brown's Farm by the beach to oppose the landing with him. He was, in fact, wrong. The British had not landed any boats when Mallet, Deshon, and Hampsted arrived. To Hempsted's surprise, there were only about forty militia there to meet them.

When the British had loaded their first set of landing boats, their warships opened up with a bombardment of the shore.

The balls flew over the heads of the militia. The British sent some of their boats further west by small creek called Lister's Gut in an apparent effort to outflank the militiamen. As soon as they landed, they formed a line of battle and made for the high ground. They soon reached a series of fences from which they exchanged volleys with the Americans. The militia were grossly outnumbered and quickly fell back toward Fort Town Hill.[39]

Among the Americans joining the militia on the beach was a young Jonathan Brooks, accompanying his father, who, like John Hempsted, had sent his family away to refuge some two and a half miles from town. He sent his two younger sons to take the family cow to a more distant pasture. Then, probably because he did not have a little black boy slave to ride his horse back, he took his eldest, but still minor son with him for the same purpose. Brooks's father apparently went toward White Beach (further west of the main landing beach). By the time the Brookses got there, the British were in the process of landing and bombarding the coast. The Brookses quickly turned around and headed inland. Before they could make it to the high ground, their horse became mired in the swampy area near Lister's Gut. Just as they extricated their horse by dismounting and moved toward higher ground, a shot cut through a thicket directly across from where they had stood a moment ago. They remounted their horse and continued up the road toward the site where it forked.

After the Royal Navy had bombarded the coast, the Americans at the landing sites withdrew and allowed the British to complete their landing unimpeded. In their traditional role as skirmishers and riflemen, the Hessian Jägers spearheaded the invasion force and pushed back the American skirmishers on the road to New London (Ocean Avenue today).

Further up that road, Jonathan Brooks and his father met up with about a hundred or so militia who were attempting to organize themselves and determine the best approach to stopping the British. The British were fast approaching in solid marching columns. It was at that time that Lieutenant Colonel Harris galloped up to the men with sword in hand. A cheer rose up and the men said to each other that now they had a commander to tell them what to do. But instead, Harris apologized to the men and declared "I have a violent sick headache this morning and can hardly sit on my horse." Then he turned and rode off without designating a commander to take his place, and without issuing any orders to the men.[40]

The Connecticut men were outraged at the colonel's abandonment of them, which they perceived as cowardice. They then turned to Nathaniel Saltonstall, a privateer captain, for leadership. The captain had earlier declared that he was not about to face the British in the road. He suggested they divide themselves into two parties and get behind the stone walls on either side of the road and try to get off a round or two off at the British or loyalists as they approached. On the New London side of the river, the vast majority of British troops were composed of provincial (loyalist) regulars. It was at this moment that Jonathan's father sent his son off with the horse to bring him back to the stable at their home and await his father's return.[41]

John Hempsted was among the militia on or near the road. He was already trading shots with Arnold's men from one stone wall to another. Hempsted and his fellow militiamen fired and retreated until they were within cannon range of what he too referred as Fort Nonsense (Fort Town Hill). The men in that fort began firing their cannon toward the loyalists, but their shots were falling short, landing near the retreating militiamen. Hempsted realized that he and his fellow militiamen were between two fires, and that unless the guns at Fort Nonsense ceased firing, he and his fellow patriots would be hit by the fort's guns. He sent one of his companions to the fort to tell them to stop the firing which they promptly did. He then moved further back toward a house by the fort. There he was accosted by the owner of the house to partake of a case of Holland gin. Hempsted was most agreeable to the invitation. He was soon joined by Captains Nathaniel Saltonstall, Richard Deshon, Jonathan Calkins , and William Coit, all of whom partook of the homeowner's generosity. Rather than leave it for the British, they took the case into a field with high weeds and bent the weeds over the case in an effort to hide it. Then they dispersed.[42]

Hempsted saw that some of the enemy were filing off the road to his right in an attempt to surround the fort from the west. Hempsted and three others elected to confront those troops by posting themselves on a hill to the northwest of the fort where they could get off some shots from an advantageous position. As Hempsted describes it, the loyalists approached in (sic) "Ingan file" (Indian file), largely masked by the mature stalks of corn, with only their bayonets showing over the stalks. Those loyalist troops were likely part of Lieutenant Colonel's Upham's 120-man battalion calling themselves the Refugees. They had been ordered with the Jägers to cover the left flank of Arnold's column approaching the town from the main road, now called Ocean Road. Hempsted waited until the British, numbering around a dozen, had reached a stone wall to his left, about thirty-three yards (six rods) distant. That's when Hempsted ordered his men to fire. The Refugees returned the fire and Hempsted's men fell back toward Fort Nonsense about 165 yards distant. Hempsted continued to trade shots, but the British ranks had grown to twelve to fifteen men, and a couple of them had jumped the wall and were fast approaching him. He describes the men as wearing green coats and feathers. That can only mean they were Jägers.

This is also supported by Captain Lyman's map, which shows the Jägers as part of the force covering Arnold's left flank.

Hempsted, with bullets whizzing by, ran toward Fort Nonsense with the enemy in hot pursuit. When he got there, it was deserted. He ran through the fort's rear entrance and into the outer ditches, all the time being fired upon by the British who had followed him into the fort. Hempsted was not giving up. As he ran into an orchard, he saw a man taunting the British with "Welcome, Goddamn you, to Fort Nonsense!" This only brought further musket shots.[43]

Hempsted headed into town. There, he heard artillery fire to the north of the town. He soon discovered about a hundred mostly unarmed militiamen on Manwaring's Hill to the northwest of the town with a 12-pounder field piece. As the British approached, the militia took flight and Hempsted and his few remaining colleagues, Captain Deshon and William Ashcroft, fired a couple of rounds from the cannon. Hempsted and his companions knew they must abandon the gun and flee, but first he told his companions that they must hide the cartridges and implements, lest the British turn the gun against them. They hid the rammers, sponges, and powder ladles under a bridge, and hid the cartridge box in the tall grass. Hempsted then went looking for something to spike the gun but came up empty. (Spiking refers to a special spike hammer-driven into the vent at the breach of the barrel of the cannon and then broken off the head of the spike, making extraction from the breach vent ,also called the touch hole, near impossible, thereby making it impossible to touch off the cannon and rendering the piece unusable.) The gun was taken by the British and never used. There was no need. The destruction of New London was already well underway.[44]

Hempsted was not done. He made his way to Quaker Hill, where he found a group of some five hundred men who were mostly unarmed and, despite the urging of their officer, failed to move any closer to the enemy. Hempsted went into New London to find his deceased father's office and retrieve some valuable papers. Then with others, he retired to a nearby swamp where many of the town's inhabitants sought shelter to wait out the storm.[45]

The Burning of
New London

After dawdling near Fort Nonsense, Jonathan Brooks made his way home and placed the horse, as ordered, in the stable. He then sat in the house located on Banks Street, which was not touched by the British, as it was known to contain mostly widow residences. He remained there till he heard a great commotion nearby. He followed some five or six shabby-looking fellows, one of whom was yelling how they were going to get plunder, racing toward the warehouses on Water Street. Perched on a fence, he saw the doors of a warehouse thrown wide open and a crowd of thirty to forty men engaged in looting. The looted goods were from the *Hannah* and were worth a fortune. Jonathan heard the anguished cries of his mother calling him home. He was handed a sack of important documents to take to his Uncle Richard's home, the appointed place of refuge for the whole family. His mother promised to follow.[46]

The street was crowded with people heading out of town with their most important possessions. When asked about the location of the British, Jonathan said the British would be upon them in five minutes if they did not hurry. That sent the crowd into a panic and they soon dropped their possessions and fled posthaste down the street. The British had already occupied Post Hill, and when Jonathan had to ride by it on Cohanzy Street, he felt a shower of bullets whizzing by his head.

He made it to his uncle's and his mother showed up an hour later. She then sent him on another errand to find his missing younger brothers. This meant returning into town.

At first, Jonathan found his way blocked by the Connecticut 20th Regiment of militia from Norwich, which had arrived and were perched on a hill overlooking the town. The regiment's colonel refused to let him go but allowed him to follow the colonel and his men toward another hill. After viewing the carnage below, they turned away toward a farm and young Jonathan, seeing his chance escaped by spurring his horse down to the town from the north. He passed onto Main Street and rode for about a hundred yards, but the heat of the burning buildings proved too much for his horse, and young Jonathan was forced to retreat back up the street beyond the burning buildings. Just as he arrived to where he thought he was safe, a warehouse filled with gunpowder exploded and surrounded young Jonathan with smoke and debris, but he escaped unharmed. He trotted down Bradley Street where his father's office was located. It was unscathed. Not finding his brothers, he rode down to State Street and the public square, which was engulfed in the conflagration. Near the printing office, he found a prostrate redcoat passed out from drink. Jonathan dismounted and removed the soldier's gun but was afraid to remove his cartridge box. He tried, but could not mount the horse with the gun, so he threw the gun over a nearby fence. At this point, Jonathan decided to leave town and head for his grandfather's house and a reunion with his family.[47]

The Fall of
Fort Trumbull

American resistance was ineffectual in impeding Arnold's approach on the straight road to New London. About two miles from the landing, the British had reached the road leading to Fort Trumbull, which forked off to the right of the high road to New London. Arnold detached four companies of the 38th regiment under Captain Millet and a company of Arnold's own American Legion under Captain Frink to attack the fort from the rear, while the van of his column continued up the road to assault Fort Nonsense.[48]

The American defenders at Fort Nonsense were in total disarray. Leaderless, the defenders had actually fired into the backs of the retreating American militia, who masked the guns of the fort and thereby prevented them from putting any effective fire on the enemy closing in on the unprotected land side of Fort Trumbull. Fort Nonsense would soon be abandoned, and with it, all organized resistance on the western side of the river collapsed.

The guns of Fort Nonsense were supposed to protect the unprotected rear of Fort Trumbull from attack. With Fort Nonsense neutralized, the four companies of the 38th regiment and the company of the American Legion could easily overwhelm the mere twenty-three-man garrison at Fort Trumbull. The garrison managed to fire grapeshot (a canvas bag filled with grape size iron projectiles) at their attackers from their three 6-pounders, which either already faced inland or could easily be turned on their field carriages. The twelve 18-pounders at the fort were probably mounted on garrison carriages, making them harder to turn around. The attackers sustained minor casualties, with four or five killed or wounded.[49]

The fort's commander, Captain Adam Shapley, realized Fort Trumbull was lost. After firing the few cannon facing inland, Shapley spiked his guns and had the garrison embark on three row boats to cross the Thames River to Fort Griswold. The British came on so quickly that the launched boats had no time to get out of musket range (about one hundred twenty five yards). The British fired several volleys at the departing boats, but fortunately for the garrison, the nearness of the boats caused the British to overshoot most of the fleeing Americans. The men in one of the boats were not so lucky and were forced to surrender, probably after several of the oarsmen were hit. Still, the seventeen men in the two remaining boats managed to make it to the eastern shore just beneath Fort Griswold. When they entered the fort through the sally port, they were greeted with cheers as deliverers. They arrived just in time to reinforce the fort with desperately needed experienced gunners.[50]

Among the Fort Trumbull survivors was one Lieutenant Richard Chapman, second-in-command of Trumbull. He had sent his two sons away with his wife and daughters before joining the garrison. Chapman was one of five brothers. One had been killed in the French and Indian War some twenty-five years earlier. Another brother, a major in the Continental Army, was killed at the Battle of Harlem Heights. The other two were at sea serving as ship captains and would thereby escape the carnage.[51]

Arnold Enters
New London

Upon taking Fort Trumbull, Arnold sent a messenger across the river to make contact with Lieutenant Colonel Eyre and urge him to take Fort Griswold as soon as possible to prevent the privateers from escaping upriver. After the landing, some local Tories told Arnold that the fort was only manned by thirty men at most and was in poor shape. Arnold wanted to assure Eyre of the fort's poor condition and small garrison. Arnold speculated that the howitzer Eyre had brought with his men should be close enough to the fort to quickly lob some shells into the heart of the fort. Howitzers are short-barreled cannon mounted on field carriages like regular field cannon, but are designed to fire at a target by firing a shell in an arc over an obstacle—like a fortress wall—to explode inside the fortification. Unlike regular field cannon, they were not designed to fire solid shot, but like field cannon, could be used to fire antipersonnel projectiles like cannister shot and grapeshot. In that way, they were very versatile by combining the ability of a mortar to fire shells over obstacles and the power of field cannon to fire directly on troops in the field with cannister and grapeshot. They were short bar-reled like mortars, but unlike mortars, they were mounted on field carriages with two large wheels and had their trunnions placed in the middle of the barrel instead of at the barrel's end. Unfortunately, Eyre's two cannon never made it to the fort until after battle was concluded.[52]

The wind that allowed the British to land on the beaches enabled many of the privateers to begin to sail upstream over the bar in the river to the safety of Norwich, Arnold's home-town. Arnold observed that the wind was light and the tide was going out, so those ships making for the bar would be forced to stop and anchor from time to time. Arnold was intent on stopping them by using the guns at Fort Griswold, but time was running out.[53]

Arnold's plan for the destruction of New London was to approach the town in two prongs, one from the north and headed by Upham's Refugees and the Jägers. The rest of Arnold's men would proceed along the river side of the town, coming up Water and Banks Streets, then moving toward the town's center to hook up with Upham's Refugees. In accordance with Arnold's plan, Upham attacked and seized the gun manned by Hempsted on Manwaring's Hill. They then went on to loot and burn Robert Manwaring's house.[54]

Arnold initially followed Upham's men. After they took pos-session of Manwaring Hill at around noon, Arnold rode up to the top of the old burial ground, which was to the northeast of Manwaring Hill and to the west of New London, to stop and surveil the harbor and New London. He paused with volun-teer aide-de-camp Lord Dalrymple and took out a spyglass. He saw the privateers moving off upriver over the bar to the north.

Upham moved the one Royal Artillery cannon landed on the west side of the Thames to the crest of a hill to the northeast of Manwaring Hill, and from there attempted to hit the escaping vessels moving upstream on the river to no avail.[55]

Arnold and his men moved into the town and made for the wharfs and warehouses on Bank Street with the intent of destroying all stores. As cited by Jonathan Brooks, many of the town's lower classes were busy looting the stores just before the redcoats arrived. Arnold claimed to have ordered his men not to loot private property or molest its inhabitants. To the extent this order was obeyed is not known, but the Jägers, being Hessian, were not above gorging themselves on the spoils of war, as evidenced by the loot found in the knapsack of one captured Jäger.[56]

After descending Manwaring's Hill, Upham's men went on to burn the town's mill and printing office at the northern edge of Winthrop's Cove. They moved on to Winthrop's Neck in an orgy of destruction that left only one private residence standing. They then went onto Main Street, where they made sure to destroy the house and stores of General Gordon Saltonstall. On Richard's Street, they prepared to burn Captain Guy Richard's home, but Richard's daughter was lying ill in the home and those taking care of her pleaded with a sympathetic Crown officer, who ordered the house be spared.[57]

Those acts of mercy were rare. At Bank Street and Water Street, important storehouses and shops were set alight. Arnold directed the destruction of ten to twelve vessels moored there, including the *Hannah*, whose capture had precipitated the raid. The *Hannah* had been partially unloaded at Shaw's wharf. She was torched and burned down almost to the water line, but not before drifting away to sink close to the end of Winthrop's Neck. One of the other vessels contained an immense cargo of gunpowder that exploded with such force that the fire was spread to additional structures by a change of wind.[58]

With the destruction of buildings and at least thirty-seven warehouses on the waterfront, the invaders moved inland to destroy all that was on the Parade, including the courthouse and jail, the Episcopal church, the old magazine and battery, and some eighteen shops and sixty-five dwellings. The vandalism encompassed the smashing of hogsheads of sugar and coffee as well as rum. Imported Irish butter melted in the flames and flowed down the gutters of the streets. Ironically, the former schoolhouse of Nathan Hale, the executed American spy and hero, escaped destruction.[59]

Even houses of loyalists were not spared. Arnold dined at the house of James Tilly, one such friend to the government, but before they could rise from the table, the house was in flames. He knew that if he spared houses of known loyalists, their neighbors would take out their anger against them, and he sought to prevent such an outcome. Arnold saved the house of his former friend, privateer Captain Elisha Hinman, but that did not dissuade Abigail Hinman from trying to shoot Arnold from an upstairs window when she saw him.[60] According to legend, the musket misfired, thus sparing the traitor's life.[61]

On the western part of Main Street lay a tavern, the proprietress of which was married to a sergeant in the militia. She was busy preparing a repast for her brother, who was serving as an officer in the loyalist Refugees. After the plates and dishes were set out on the table, she met up with her husband, who had been busy skirmishing with the approaching loyalists, and rode off with him just one step ahead of the enemy. Upon entering the town, her brother made for his sister's establishment, and there refreshed himself with his fellow officers. The house was not touched, and years later, her Tory brother received permission to visit his sister at the tavern where he soon after died.[62]

The houses on Bradley Street, also known as Widows' Row, were also spared due to the want of stores and shops and the presence of widows. Where residents remained and begged the soldiers to spare their homes, they were often successful in saving their houses.[63]

Thirty miles north of New London in the town of New Scotland, the congregation of Dr. James Cogswell were alarmed by the sound of cannon and the reddened sky to the south.[64] They had nothing to fear. Arnold had no intention to go further in-land. The British had accomplished their goal of destroying New London.

By four o'clock, the British succeeded in inflicting enormous damage upon the town. They destroyed some 143 buildings. Ninety-seven families were made homeless. The monetary loss was placed at an enormous sum of 151,606 pounds.[65]

The Approach to
Fort Griswold

While Arnold was debarking his half of the expeditionary force on the western shore of the Thames, Lieutenant Colonel Edmund Eyre of the 54th was landing the rest
of the expedition on the eastern shore of the mouth of the
Thames River. This portion of the expedition consisted of the
40th and 54th regiments, the 3rd Battalion of the New Jersey
Volunteers (loyalists), a company of Jägers, and two guns of
the Royal Artillery with their crews. The Jägers landed first and
secured the beach.

Unlike the western shore, the landing was uncontested. Ledyard had not sent any troops to contest the landing or even to
harass the crown forces on their three-mile march to the fort.
Ledyard wanted as many men as he could have in Fort Griswold.
Continental Army Captain Amos Stanton, who had years of battlefield experience, knew the reluctance of many of the militia
to be trapped in a confined space. He wanted to fight the British

at the beach and conduct a fighting retreat toward the fort, but Ledyard and the other officers would not hear of it. Still, Ledyard was worried. He knew he didn't have nearly enough men to properly defend the fort.[66]

The roads, or rather paths, to Fort Griswold were rougher and more circuitous than the road on western shore to Fort Town Hill. Eyre was running behind, and the more direct path was too difficult to manhandle the two cannon. (No horses or oxen to draw the field pieces were embarked on the expedition.) Eyre decided to rush up with the two regiments of regulars and the Jägers and leave the smaller 3rd Battalion of the New Jersey Volunteers (150 men) to accompany the slow-moving guns. The Jägers would be useful in covering the flanks and the front of the British marching columns. Later, they would be stationed north of the fort on the road to Stonington, the nearest town to east, no doubt to intercept any relief column coming from the north or east.[67]

Eyre forced a boy herding cattle in the area into service as a guide. At ten o'clock, his advance column moved off on the cart path leading to the fort. He pushed his seven-hundred-plus force more than two miles and arrived at Avery Hill, about a half of a mile to the southeast corner of Fort Griswold. Avery Hill was the last natural barrier before the fort. It featured a ledge of rocks to shield the invasion force from destructive fire from the fort. It had taken Eyre nearly two hours to get there with the 40th and 54th regiments. His artillery, consisting of a howitzer and 6-pounder field cannon and their crews and the New Jersey loyalist 3rd battalion were still a long way off. The howitzer with its wide mouth and stubby barrel would allow them to lob shells into the fort to hopefully explode in the interior of such a fortification and cause many casualties to the garrison normally safely ensconced within its walls.[68]

Arnold had earlier sent orders to Eyre to attack the fort as soon as possible. At the time, Arnold was in the process of attacking the rear of Fort Trumbull and was witnessing American ships in harbor escaping upriver. He reasoned that if Eyre seized Fort Griswold, he could prevent those ships from escaping upriver. But it was already too late. After Arnold took Fort Nonsense, he ascended a hill to the northeast of Manwaring Hill to place his single 6- pounder to bear on the rebel ships still in the harbor. (The hill can be clearly identified on Captain Lyman's map.) Upon arriving at the hill's summit, Arnold took out his spyglass and looked out across the river to Fort Griswold. What he saw shocked him. The fort was in much better shape than he had been led to believe. It was complete and intact, and, what's more, it appeared to be fully manned. He saw that it was far too late to prevent the crewed ships in the river from escaping. Nothing of strategic worth was to be gained that would merit the incurring of the high casualties it would take to storm the fort. He immediately issued instructions to an aide to countermand his earlier attack order. It would take time to deliver that countermand. The aide would have to go down to the river and secure a boat to cross it. The river at that location was almost a mile wide, and time was running out.

Photo taken from the site of Ft. Trumbull site looking across the mile wide Thames River towards Ft. Griswold located at the Fort Griswold Monument obelisk in the center.

Parley

Meanwhile Eyre sent out Captain Beckwith of the 54th with a red flag to demand surrender of the fort. When Beckwith came within two hundred yards of the fort, a musket shot stopped him. Ledyard dispatched Captains Amos Stanton, Elijah Avery, and John Williams with their own flag. Beckwith delivered Eyre's written summons to surrender. The captains returned to the fort and deliberations began in a council of war among Ledyard and his officers. Ledyard knew that most of his force was raw and poorly trained militia. His numbers were really insufficient, and stretching his meager force to cover the walls would be impossible. Moreover, parts of the ditch on the north and east sides of the fort were caving in, there were gaps in the abatis, the gun platforms were rotting, and there were no prepared artillery cartridges.[69]

Benadem Gallup of the 8th regiment of militia based in Groton, Stonington, and Preston was in the fort. The greater part of that regiment was missing. However, he could see them gathering a few hundred yards to the north. He told Ledyard not to accede to British demands and that he would bring what appeared to be between two and three hundred men to reinforce the garrison in the fort in due course. Ledyard knew he would have a good chance of holding the post with such numbers, so he authorized Gallup to go and bring in those men. While Gallup made his way north toward the gathering militia, Ledyard sent the captains back out with his rejection of the British call to surrender.[70]

This parley took the better part of an hour. While the parley was going on, Fort Griswold was exchanging cannon fire with the British at Fort Trumbull. Apparently, Captain Shapley did not have sufficient time to spike all of Trumbull's guns or the spiking was performed imperfectly and the British were able to retract the spikes from the touch holes. With their elevated position on Groton Heights, the 12-pounders of Fort Griswold easily reached Fort Trumbull, whereas the heavier 18-pounders at Fort Trumbull could not be elevated to return the fire. Their shots fell short.[71]

After receiving Ledyard's response, Beckwith withdrew and then returned in a few minutes, but this time he advanced only to around 350 yards from the fort. The rebel captains went out again to meet him. Beckwith delivered a message that the British were prepared to storm the fort, and if they did, martial law would apply. That meant that the entire garrison would be put to the sword, all in accordance with the rules of war. Ledyard's final response was not long in coming. His final reply would leave no doubt that he was determined to hold the fort; "We will not give up the fort, let the consequences be what they may." The one-hour parley was over. The killing was about to begin. Beckwith signaled Eyre to commence the assault.[72]

This picture is taken from the approximate position of the 9-pounder in the NW bastion.

The Cannon of
Fort Griswold

Ledyard looked to the north and saw that the militia Gallup had promised to reinforce the garrison had not budged. Ledyard was going to have to make do with what he had, which was at that point somewhere between 158 and 165 men. He had detached a few men to temporarily crew the three guns at the flèche 120 yards east outside the eastern wall of the fort.

According to Faden's engraved map of the fort based on Ensign Alexander Gray's hand-drawn map, there appear to be six cannon that faced east (the land side) and could be used to contest a general assault from that direction. Two other pieces faced north and south, respectively. We can surmise from the engraved map's representation of the cannon based on the length of the lines representing the cannon barrels that the majority (ten) of the heavier pieces (12-pounders) were mounted *en barbette* (no embrasures) on the west wall facing the New London harbor. The Northwest bastion appears to hold heavier pieces also (four) but mounted at embrasures, which afforded greater protection to the men serving the pieces. Two bastion guns faced west, another one faced north, and the other pointed east along the line of the ditch before the northern curtain wall. In such a position, it would enfilade any attacker against that wall. Royal Artillery Captain John Lemoine reported that there were fourteen garrison-mounted 12-pounders in the fort. Three, if not four, must have been in the northwest bastion.[73]

Arnold in his official after battle report to Clinton that a nine-pounder enfiladed the troops attacking the southern curtain wall. In his hand-drawn map of the fort Ensign Gray of the 40th regiment indicated that there were up to three guns that "annoyed ye troops," two of which enfiladed the lines before the north and south walls, respectively. There were two 9-pounders in the fort. It is probable that the two enfilading pieces were placed in the eastern flanks of each bastion where the bastions connected with the southern and northern curtain walls. From those interior corners of the two bastions, the 9-pounders were perfectly sited to spray deadly projectiles at attackers attempting to scale the northern and southern curtain walls. There was one 18-pounder, by far the largest cannon in the fort. It was probably the gun pictured on the Faden map with a long barrel in the fort's southeast corner, facing south. This would allow it to cover the British approach from the south. The pieces facing directly east on the eastern wall appear to have shorter barrels and must be one of the five smaller-barreled types of cannon (6-pounders or less). There was a 12-pounder mounted on a traveling carriage not accounted for, which I believe could be the longer barreled gun facing north on the north wall. There, it would cover the approach to the north gate from the east and north.

The problem with manning all these cannon is that it required a well-trained and drilled artillery crew of no fewer than four men supported by a fifth person, normally a boy to run rounds to the men manning the front of the gun. Of the forts' defenders, there were a mere forty or fewer men of the garrisons of the two forts remaining who arguably had the training and experience to service the cannon, and not all of them would be available to do so (such as the officers). The volunteers from the privateers likely had experience serving cannon also but there were not many of such sailor volunteers in the fort.

Two of each gun crew would be stationed near the muzzle of the cannon barrel. The one on the left would hold an implement call a "worm," which consisted of spiral-twisted wires mounted on a long pole. The man on the right side of each cannon's mouth would be holding the combination sponge and rammer, with the sponge mounted on the top of the pole and the rammer at the bottom. To the rear of the barrel on the right side near the breach would be the man in charge of priming the touch hole with fine priming powder contained in a powder horn or flask slung over his shoulder. He would also carry the pick (a long metal sharpened pin with a ring on the unsharpened end for grapping the pick from its leather holder on the over the shoulder belt) for pricking open the canvas bag in the barrel containing the gunpowder for the round through the touch hole at the breech. That man would also carry the all-important leather thumb stall for blocking air from entering the barrel through the touch hole. Finally, the crewmember to the left would be in charge of the igniting the priming powder in the vent with either the lit slow match (twine dipped in saltpeter) wrapped on a forked metal stick called a linstock or a device called a porte fire, something comparable to an emergency flare. It was very important for the holder of the porte fire or linstock to keep the lit end of his implement away from the primed vent of the barrel—and, obviously, any other source of gunpowder. The fifth crewmember (often a boy) would be supplying the rounds, usually from several feet to the rear of the cannon.

In the field, there was often an officer in charge of aiming the cannon by adjusting the elevation of the barrel or by using a handspike to turn the gun. That would not be necessary in this battle given the point-blank ranges.

In the field, there would also be a group of men called matrosses whose job it was to use ropes to return the cannon to its original firing position after it had recoiled to the rear. There was no need of such men in the closed space of the fort. The crew itself would have to manhandle the cannon back into its position in the embrasure.

Ultimately, everything the crew did had to be done quickly and smoothly, but with a full appreciation of the terrible risks attendant to the loading and firing of these beastly weapons. In the process of firing a cannon using black powder, there almost always remained residue in the barrel from the incomplete burning of the powder charge and canvas bag in which the round was contained. The slightest ember remaining in the barrel would set off the cannon while the new round was being loaded, often costing the crew member holding the rammer both his arm and the rammer, thereby disabling the cannon. Making sure the barrel held no nasty surprises was the first job in the process of readying the cannon for loading its next round. This task involved the worming of the piece by inserting the worm into the barrel in an effort to remove large pieces of debris from the previous discharge—normally pieces of the canvas bag. After worming, the gunner holding the sponge would, after wetting it using the water in the bucket near the muzzle, clean out the barrel with the sponge. This would not be done until the man with the thumb stall near the breach had placed his thumb (using the leather thumb stall) over the tough hole to seal it. That way, air couldn't get in when the sponger extracted the sponge from the barrel. Without air, any remaining embers would be exinguished. The gunners listened for a popping sound when the sponge was removed, which indicated the creation of a partial vacuum thanks to the primer's thumb stall sealing the touch hole. After all these steps had been taken, it was reasonably safe for the next round to be rammed into the barrel for the next discharge, but not completely.

In the eighteenth century, cannon barrels were cast in brass, bronze, or iron. The black powder used to discharge weapons contained sulfur, a key ingredient that, which exposed to water, can produce sulfuric acid. That acid, however weak it may be, gradually eats away at the interior of metal cannon barrels, thereby creating crevices where embers maybe hidden and unextinguished by the techniques described above. Iron is far more susceptible to this wear than either bronze or brass. That is why experienced gunners would try to swap out their iron pieces with those made of brass or bronze. The greater part of the cannon at Fort Griswold were made of iron. All of this made loading and firing a cannon dangerous work.

Even today, with advanced metallurgy in the production of replicas of such cannon barrels, there are unfortunate incidences of reenactors losing hands and arms from premature discharges.

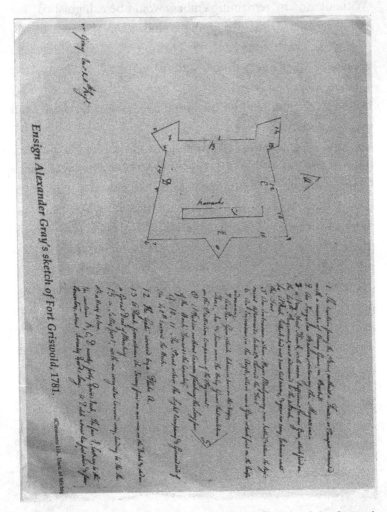

Alexander Gray's map outline, pen and ink ground plan of the fort with a detailed description of the work and places at which important incidents occurred during the British assault of September 6, 1781. *William L. Clements Library, University of Michigan.*

First Blood

Lyman map insert showing angle attack of the British 54th Reg.

Behind Avery Hill and its rocks and ledges, Eyre had hatched a plan of assault. He would take his 54th regiment and attack the southwestern corner of the fort while Major William Montgomery would assault the northeastern corner with his 40th regiment. The intent was to narrow the troops' exposure to the fort's guns. The troops had no scaling ladders and worse, no axes to cut through any abatis, ditch stockade, or fraising. To get around to the southwest bastion, Eyre would have to run the gauntlet of an 18-pounder commanded by Sergeant Hempstead from the Fort Trumbull garrison and privateer Captain Halsey, who aimed the piece.[74] The 18-pounder was loaded with two bags of grapeshot (a thick canvas bag filled with one-ounce iron balls corded together in the form of a cylinder). In a day before the modern era, grapeshot—along with canister shot—was the nearest thing to a weapon of mass destruction. We can assume that all the guns that could bear on the British assault would have been similarly loaded. Depending on the caliber, the range for such a shot was anywhere from three hundred yards for the smaller pieces to twice that for the larger pieces.

Major Montgomery of the 40th led his men in a solid column toward the flèche and the northern and eastern sides of the fort. His men would be the first to reach the fort's defenses. Along a rock ledge near the eastern brow of the ridge upon which the fort was situated sat the flèche containing up to three 4-pounders. The flèche was about 125 yards from the fort's eastern walls. The four-pounders were small, obsolete French or Swedish cannon capable of firing four-pound cannon balls. All of the patriot soldiers that had been sent out to load the pieces with grapeshot had undoubtedly already retired to the fort but for two soldiers, Captain Elijah Bailey and another member of the garrison named Williams. Their job was to fire the cannon in the flèche at the approach of the enemy and inflict as much damage as possible to the columns assaulting the eastern wall. The 40th came up in a run at trail arms at the flèche. Bailey and Williams fired the cannon and then Williams scrambled back to the fort's north gate. Sergeant Avery claimed that the cannon inflicted significant casualties on the 40th but did not appreciably slow down their assault.[75]

Like any good artillerist, in order to prevent the enemy using the guns against the fort, Bailey stayed long enough to spike the cannon by hammering spikes into the cannon's touch holes or vents. He then would break off the head of the spike to make it almost impossible to extract the spike from the touch hole. The British were close when Bailey completed the task and ran from the flèche to follow Williams to the fort. By the time he rounded the northeast corner of the fort, the gate to the fort was shut, and the British were coming up fast behind him. He continued running past the closed gate, past the Northwest Bastion, and down the slope of the ridge toward the river. As he kept looking to get out of harm's way, he saw a cornfield off on his right on the downhill slope. He quickly ran through the late summer tall corn and prostrated himself somewhere in the center of the cornfield in the hope that none of the British attackers would follow him. There he lay, hidden and undisturbed, for the rest of the day.[76]

Even as Bailey and Williams were firing the guns in the flèche, reinforcements to the fort continued to trickle in. Joseph Moxley Sr. and his nineteen-year-old carpenter son, Joseph "Joe" Moxley Jr., entered through the north gate. Joseph Moxley Sr. was the last defender to enter through the gate. After the gate was closed, militiaman Andrew Billings from North Groton (now the town of Ledyard) arrived at the fort. As he was recognized by his fellow soldiers in the fort, a rope was thrown to him to allow him entry, undoubtedly on the unfraised western wall.

As Bailey was making his run, another volunteer, John Clark, had just beached his rowboat at the foot of the hill beneath the fort. After resistance collapsed in New London, he had laboriously rowed across the river to Groton with a bag of musket cartridges. He quickly climbed the hill to the fort's western wall. A rope was likewise thrown to him, but as he climbed to enter the fort, he was shot down by the British. John Clark was the first Fort Griswold defender to fall.[77]

Meanwhile southeast of the fort, the 54th was funneling in a solid column through a gate at a stone wall bordering a wood to begin their assault on the south side of the fort. In the southeast corner lay the fort's only 18-pounder, the largest gun in the fort. It was manned by seasoned soldiers under Sergeant Hempstead of the Fort Trumbull garrison and sailors under privateer Captain Halsey. Halsey directed the gun and waited for the column to present itself in the perfect position for maximum impact. That first shot struck the redcoat column with devastating effect. The bodies of twenty British regulars were strewn about, and the column left in disarray. They broke up into platoons and fired their muskets at the defenders as they moved west. Some men headed due west for the southwest bastion while others may have headed north for the eastern and northern walls.[78]

South Wall near SE corner looking east. On the ramparts to the left would have been the embrasure from which the 18-pounder fired grape shot on the 54th Regiment.

Close view of the fort's north entrance and the eastern flank and face of the northwest bastion. A 9-pounder would have been in place on the flank of the bastion to enfilade the north curtain wall.

Small Arms and Pikes

Inside the fort, the men on the ramparts stepped up onto the firing step. They made ready to fire upon the enemy over the parapet when they got within effective range of their notoriously inaccurate smoothbore muskets. A common terminology mistake is to confuse muskets with rifles. A rifle refers to a weapon with a rifled barrel, where the interior of the barrel is etched or cut with a series of spiraling grooves intended on making the bullet spin in a uniform way, thereby increasing its range and accuracy. Rifles would not become standard-issue to soldiers until the 1850s. There were no rifled weapons with the Americans at Fort Griswold to our knowledge.

A common musket of the American Revolution had a maximum effective range of two hundred yards, but as Major George Hanger is quoted as saying, you might as well fire at the moon as fire at a man at two hundred yards. In tests conducted in Britain in the 1740s on the accuracy of the standard musket of the British army, it was noted that only one aimed shot in two fired at a man-size target at one hundred meters hit home. More modern tests of such weapons yielded even worse results at fifty yards (one out of five).[79] A smoothbore musket was like a giant shotgun. It was devastatingly effective at short range, especially if the musket ball cartridge included three additional pieces of buckshot (buck and ball). It was no wonder that Israel Putnam ordered his men at the Battle of Bunker Hill to hold their fire against the British until they could see the whites of their eyes.

We don't know how most of the soldiers in the fort were distributed. Those bearing muskets would likely have been arranged in pairs with one loading while the other fired. The regular members of the garrisons of Forts Trumbull and Griswold undoubtedly manned the cannon. Sailors from the privateers were also probably assigned to man the cannon. As the flintlock musket was subject to frequent misfires and a high degree of inaccuracy and because it was single shot and required at least fifteen seconds to load and fire in the most ideal of circumstances, hand-to-hand combat could be expected. The fort was well supplied with some eighty half pikes for such close fighting.[80] The half pikes being eight feet in length would easily outreach the British eighteen-inch bayonets affixed upon five-foot muskets. Ledyard probably had a reserve of reliable men armed with eight-foot half pikes on the fort's parade ground to act as a mobile reserve force ready to plug any breach in the fort's defenses. Ledyard was reported by others as being on the parade ground during the battle probably accompanied by his pike-bearing black orderly Jordan Freeman. Nevertheless, the British regulars were very proficient in the use of the bayonet, whereas the Americans were not with the exception of the men of the Continental line of whom there were few present.

The bayonet was a nasty lethal weapon so much worse because it was up close and personal. The bayonet of that era had a triangular-shaped spearhead, intended to make a wound that would be hard to close. Moreover, two of the three sides of the bayonet contained indented channels to allow blood to flow freely around the sides of the bayonet imbedded in the victim's body thereby facilitating extraction of the bayonet from the victim's body so the attacker could use the weapon again and again.

Eyre's Assault
and Wounding

A s the 54th began their run to the southwest bastion, they must have run the gauntlet of musket fire and the continuing fire of the 18-pounder strategically placed on the south wall. The 40th undoubtedly ran into the same heavy fire as they approached the east and north walls. The abatis and ditch would have slowed them down and made them better targets as well as any palisade that may have bordered the outside of the ditch or curtain wall. If the British made it through the abatis and any outer palisade to the ditch or ground before the north and south walls, they would find themselves directly in the path of the muzzles of the two 9-pounders placed in the flanks of the two bastions to enfilade the entire British line before the north and south walls.

The Patriots put up a fierce resistance, though the many young and inexperienced volunteer militia must have been fearful at the number of enemies assaulting their positions. Others, in contrast, brave by virtue of inexperience, foolishly exposed themselves by mounting the parapet to get a better shot at the attackers. Encouraged by his friend, John Morgan stood upon the parapet to fire on the enemy advancing to the walls. This risky move, while affording him a better position to fire down upon the British under the walls, completely exposed his body to British musket fire. Morgan soon found himself crippled by a British musket ball to his knee.[81] It must have been with some relief that after a time the British pulled back, apparently in response to the serious wounding of their division's commander, Lieutenant Colonel Eyre.

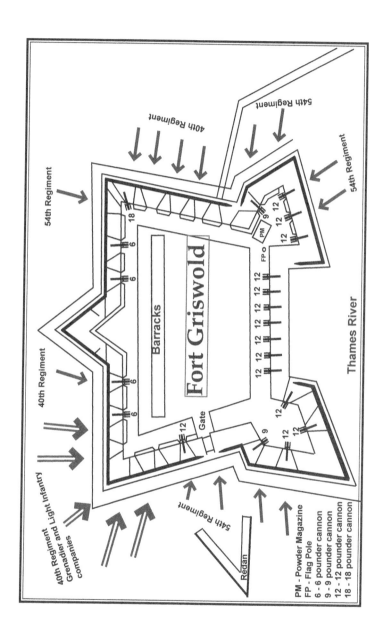

The Flag Goes Down

After Eyre's wounding, Major Montgomery of the 40th moved to the south of the fort to assume overall command. He may have taken with him at least some of the companies of the 40th, but not the light and grenadier companies. During this lull, Montgomery considered calling off the assault. He must have seen that New London was ablaze and the ships remaining in the harbor captured. It was too late to stop the manned ships that escaped upriver. Taking the fort no longer served any purpose. Then something happened which changed everything.

One of the British soldiers, or perhaps a Jäger, decided to take a parting shot at some patriot in the southwest bastion. The shot missed its intended target and instead severed the halyard on the fort's flagstaff, causing the fort's thirteen-striped flag to fall to the ground.

The lowering of a ship's or fort's flag in the eighteenth century meant the fort was being surrendered. Patriot Luke Perkins reacted almost immediately. He grabbed one of the eighty half pikes, quickly tied the flag to the pike, and planted the pike on the bastion's ramparts so the enemy might know that the fort was not being surrendered. However quickly he may seemingly have acted, it was not fast enough.[82]

The dispirited British soldiers saw the flag was down and concluded that the Americans had had enough and were surrendering. They began to walk to the fort in a jubilant mood. When the stunned and dismayed defenders saw the British advancing, they unleashed a barrage of shot. Now it was time for the British to react. To them, the rebels had perpetrated a dirty trick. The deceitful Americans had lowered their flag to lure the British into coming within the range of their guns. Such perfidious behavior from the cowardly Americans was to be expected. It had been done years before at the Battle of Brooklyn in August of 1776, when some of Washington's riflemen clubbed their rifles (turning their guns upside down, muzzle facing the ground as a sign of surrender) only to bring them up and fire when the unsuspecting British came close to round up their prisoners. The British and Hessians' response to such perfidy was to refuse to accept the surrender of any riflemen and instead to skewer their captives on the point of their bayonets, sometimes impaling them on trees. The surviving men of the 54th and 40th regiments became enraged and pressed their assault with a bitter resolve that the Americans should face full retribution for their treachery.[83]

Shows the southwest faces of the southwest bastion from the view of the attackers. It shows the flag location and the boulder on the left at the meeting point of the two faces of the bastion. Note the steepness of the approach.

The Attack Renewed
Under Montgomery

The assault focused on all sides of the fort save the west but the strongest effort appears to have been made on the south side where there was no ditch. The British on that side were led by the 40th's commander, Major Montgomery. The British continued to encounter fierce resistance as they advanced toward the fort's walls. The attackers fought their way through the abatis and any outer palisade to get to the ground (south wall) or ditch before the walls on the north and east walls as well as the two riverside bastions.

Those before the north and south walls faced the deadly enfilade from the two 9-pounders. Perhaps as often as every twenty seconds, a blast of canister from those two 9-pounders at point-blank range could take out a dozen or more of the regulars in their path. Other cannon along the same walls facing north and south, respectively, toward the east end of the south and north walls, would inflict damage to those attackers nearest the embrasure from which the muzzles of those cannon protruded.[84]

The American gunners could not maximize their rate of fire for want of prepared charges. This meant that fire workers in the magazine (artillerymen in charge of preparing cartridges) would have to measure out the gunpowder and attach the projectile (grapeshot or canister) as they went instead of having them prepared in advance. A young boy or young man assigned to each manned cannon (and called a powder monkey on ships) would be tasked with running the cartridges up to each of the operating cannon. This was a time-consuming process, particularly given the many different calibers of cannon. This was because a 6-pounder was not going to take a cartridge intended for a 12-pounder and vice versa, and there were at least six different calibers of cannon in the fort.

The British had their own difficulties to overcome. To mount the walls without scaling ladders and axes, the British soldiers would have to pair up, with one soldier supporting another's attempt to dislodge the twelve-foot pointed wooden stakes of the fraise perhaps by hoisting his comrade on his shoulders so he could reach the stakes protruding six to eight feet from the earthen walls above the lower stone portion of the rampart. This was done in an attempt to jiggle loose and dislodge the stakes. While the British regulars were attempting this difficult task, they were being fired on by the cannon and muskets of the defenders. Other British soldiers would stand behind the men trying to dislodge the fraising or pickets and fire at the defenders as they raised their heads and arms above the parapet to fire on the men beneath the wall. At the very least, such fire would cause the defenders to fire in haste and disturb the defenders' aim. One defender, Private John Daboll of the 8th Connecticut regiment (militia), dueled with a particular British soldier beneath the wall. Daboll fired seven times at him, missing him despite the short range. The duel ended when the Brit's shot took off the lock of Daboll's musket and wounded him in the head and hand.[85]

On the south wall near the southeast corner, Sergeant Hempstead from Fort Trumbull was maneuvering the big eighteen-pounder into the embrasure before which it was positioned. Every time a cannon was fired, the recoil would push the gun back a few feet, which enabled the crew to reload the piece from the muzzle. The cannon then had to be manhandled forward so that the muzzle was inserted back into the embrasure to fire. As this was being done, a British soldier managed to put a one-ounce musket ball through the temporarily open embrasure, where it cut into one of Hempstead's ears. The wound bled profusely. The sergeant had to stop and tie a handkerchief around the wound on his head to stanch the bleeding.[86]

View of the Southwest Bastion from the rampart of the South Wall looking southwest towards the Thames River and Fort Trumbull. The site of the water battery can be see in the middle left of the photograph.

The Breach of the Southwest Bastion

The Americans were inflicting horrendous casualties on the attackers, in part due to the 9-pounders in the eastern flanks of the bastions. British officers realized that the enfilading cannon in the southwest bastion had to be taken out if the south wall were to be taken. The 54th concentrated many men against the southwest bastion to exploit a fatal weakness in its construction: the incorporation of a large boulder embedded on its western side. That boulder, which can be seen today, disallowed the placement of a fraise and shielded an attacker from the musket fire of the defenders because of its almost perpendicular angle. One by one, the British regulars climbed onto the parapet by means of the boulder and swarmed into the bastion. They took on the men manning the cannon from the rear. Captain Richards and Lieutenant Chapman were slain; Captain Shapley, the refugee commander of Fort Trumbull, was mortally wounded.

Fighting in the southwest bastion were Sergeant Avery, Luke Perkins, John and Stephen Whittlesey, Joseph Moxley. Sr. and Andrew Gallup. John Whittlesey was shot in the head. Moxley was mortally wounded by a bayonet to the gut. In all the confusion, at least one British soldier made it all the way to the front gate and tried to open it. He failed and was slain.[87]

As the fire from the southwest bastion slackened, the British renewed their assault on the south wall. They began to dislodge the pickets, thereby creating openings in the fraise. Then, one man at a time might squeeze through the gap with the boost provided by his fellow soldiers and mount on to the remaining pickets as they made their way to the open embrasures where no cannon were placed. Twenty-one-year-old Samuel Edgecomb probably grew frustrated with the inability to fire often enough on the attackers as they made openings in the fraise. He got a hold of the iron round shot intended for the eighteen-pounder. There was no need for such long-range ammunition in this fight. Picking up one eighteen-pound round shot in each hand, he hurled the iron balls on the heads of the attackers beneath the ramparts. At some point, probably while he exposed himself as he hurled the balls, Samuel was wounded in one of his hands.[88]

In the southeast corner of the ramparts, the wounded Sergeant Stephen Hempstead, a veteran of Bunker Hill, exhibited the cool determination of a veteran as he continued to fire and load his cannon to the last. He saw a head of a British soldier poking through an opening in the fraise in front of the cannon to Hempstead's left. The Brit cried out to the neighboring gun crew "My brave fellows, the enemy are breaking in behind you." Hempstead noticed that to a man, the gun crew had turned around to look at the maelstrom in the Southwest Bastion. Hempstead grabbed a pike and thrust it at the soldier's protruding head. At that very moment, he was shot in the arm bearing the pike. He quickly switched to the other (right) arm and thrust the pike at the Brit. He was joined by the gun crew and the soldier ducked his head below the fraising to escape injury.[89]

The two gun crews in the southeast corner continued to operate. Andrew Gallup, one of the original garrison with one of the three guns along the south wall or southwest bastion, continued to operate his cannon until the boy, fifteen-year-old Daniel Williams, acting in his role as a powder monkey, failed to return with new rounds for the gun. Williams was a substitute for a soldier from Trumbull's garrison, who lived many miles west of New London in the town of Old Saybrook at the mouth of the Connecticut River. A few days earlier, a Fort Trumbull soldier had been given temporary leave to see his sick wife. Because his wife needed him, he went to his neighbors to find a temporary replacement. At some point, he approached Daniel's father and offered him a hogshead of cider if he would send young Daniel as his replacement. Mr. Williams gladly accepted the trade and sent his boy off for what he must have assumed would be an uneventful interlude in New London's Fort Trumbull.[90]

When Andrew Gallup looked around for Williams, he saw that the boy had been shot on his way to or from the powder magazine. As Gallup was staring at the body, he was struck in the hip by a shot through the embrasure. Gallup fell disabled. His comrades carried him down the platform to the parade ground facing north.[91]

As the cannon in the southwest bastion were silenced and openings in the fraise were made and widened on the south wall and the embrasures cleared of defenders by British musket fire, Major Montgomery seized the moment to lead his men through the unoccupied central or third embrasure in the south wall. As he climbed into the open embrasure and rose to beckon his soldiers to follow, he was impaled on a pike wielded by Jordan

Freeman, Colonel Ledyard's steadfast orderly. Montgomery was killed by the thrust. Command would now devolve onto Major Stephen Bromfield of the 54th.[92]

Simultaneous with the breakthroughs on the south wall and southwest bastion, the light and grenadier companies of the 40th had managed to climb through the unoccupied embrasures in the northeast corner and overwhelm the garrison on that part of the fort.

As more and more British climbed through the embrasures and over the parapets, the defenders fought fiercely. Captain William Latham and his slave Lambo loaded and fired as quickly as they could until Lambo was slain and Captain William Latham wounded in the thigh. Lieutenant Parke Avery fought side by side with his seventeen-year-old son, Thomas. He urged Thomas to do his duty and watched him die, one of nine Avery's to be slain that day. One British soldier who climbed onto the parapet from the fraising stood up and thrust down with his bayonet into the lieutenant's forehead, exposing his brain and taking out one of his eyes. Left for dead, the lieutenant would survive to live to the ripe old age of eighty-one.[93]

Location of the 9-pounder in the SW Bastion.

Shows the plaque placed at the position on the interior of the south wall near the location of the embrasure where Major Montgomery met his end on the point of a half pike wielded by Colonel Ledyard's black servant, Jordan Freeman.

Looking north along the eastern wall from the wedged shape projection in its center. It would have been in the northeastern corner that the grenadiers and light infantry of the 40th Foot entered the fort.

View of the fort's interior from the vantage point of the north gate entrance and looks upon south wall and the SW Bastion on the right.

Breakthrough and Slaughter

Eventually in the confusion, one of the British soldiers made it to the north entrance and succeeded in opening the fort's double-gated north entrance. When that happened, a tide of brick red swept onto the northern part of the fort's parade ground. From there, the Brits mounted the parapet, probably on the western and northern walls. Then, according to Sergeant Avery, they turned as one and fired down on the Americans still on the ramparts. They began to sweep the ramparts of defenders from the western wall. Sergeant Rufus Avery was standing only five feet away from Captain Edward Latham and Christopher Latham, a crewman from the *Hancock*, when he saw the British knock them down and bayonet Edward. When a soldier went to bayonet Christopher, Christopher grabbed the man and would have thrown him down but was shot in the forearm and the man escaped. Now helpless, he was attacked by another soldier wielding his musket like a club. That soldier knocked him senseless.

For the rest of Christopher's life, he would carry that musket ball lodged in his forearm.[94]

Sergeant Avery, whose coat had a bullet hole and a rip from a bayonet thrust, fled the Southwest Bastion for the supposed safety of the barracks on the east side of the fort. The British were now advancing toward the south end of the parade in three platoons, firing volleys at every American in their path. In response to the British breakthrough, some defenders had fled into the barracks and were firing on the British from its windows.

Avery reached the barracks door unscathed only to witness the British firing into the windows of the barracks. As he turned around to flee the barracks, he saw Colonel Ledyard's body lying at the feet of a British officer. Before Sergeant Avery could run from the barracks door, he was caught by a soldier who yelled that he would "skipper him bejesus." Avery begged for his life all the while soldier tried three times to stab him with his bayonet. Being unsuccessful he gave up the attempt and spared poor Sergeant Avery. Others were not so lucky. Captain William Seymour, another of Ledyard's nephews, was shot in the knee. Then, as he lay helpless on the ground, he was bayoneted thirteen times. Rufus also watched as the British slew the regular garrison's second-in-command Lieutenant Enoch Stanton just a few feet from him.[95]

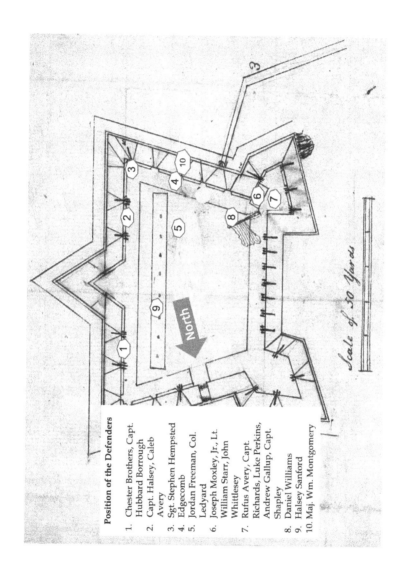

Position of the Defenders

1. Chester Brothers, Capt. Hubbard Borrough
2. Capt. Halsey, Caleb Avery
3. Sgt. Stephen Hempsted
4. Edgecomb
5. Jordan Freeman, Col. Ledyard
6. Joseph Moxley, Jr., Lt. William Starr, John Whittlesey
7. Rufus Avery, Capt. Richards, Luke Perkins, Andrew Gallup, Capt. Shapley
8. Daniel Williams
9. Halsey Sanford
10. Maj. Wm. Montgomery

Scale of 30 Yards

Surrender and the Slaying of Colonel Ledyard

Colonel Ledyard knew the situation was hopeless and ordered his men to put down their weapons as he made his way with his orderly Jordan Freeman to the north end of the parade toward a British officer identified as either Captain Beckwith or Major Bromfield in order to surrender the fort. Beckwith was a captain of the 54th regiment who, prior to the assault, tried to negotiate a surrender of the fort in the parley. Sergeant Avery claimed that he saw Ledyard approach the officer at the north end of the fort's parade ground near the fort's open gate. As the story is told by Stephen Hempstead, Ledyard approached Major Bromfield to surrender his sword. Bromfield supposedly asked, "Who commands the fort?" In response, Ledyard said, "I did Sir, but you do now." Then Ledyard unsheathed and tendered his sword, hilt first, to Bromfield, who seized the sword and immediately thrust it into Ledyard's torso. Who was there to witness this exchange and outrage besides Hempstead is not at all clear.[96]

Avery suggested that it was Captain Buskirk of the New Jersey Provincials who was approached by Ledyard. This is improbable as the Provincials were just arriving in the vicinity of the fort, probably too late to participate in the assault.

After the slaying of Ledyard, his orderly Jordan Freeman and Ledyard's thirty-year-old nephew Captain Youngs Ledyard supposedly rushed into the fray to defend or avenge the slaying of the colonel. They, in turn, were bayoneted. Freeman was killed outright and the captain mortally wounded.

Dr. Walter Powell in his 2000 publication *Murder or Mayhem?* suggests that Hempstead's 1826 narrative, written when Hempstead was seventy-two years old, is an outright fabrication or embellishment of Hempstead's original reports of the battle to Governor Trumbull back on September 30, 1781. In his 1782 deposition, he wrote only that the British put to death a great number of the garrison as well as Colonel Ledyard while they were begging for quarter.[97]

This appears to be corroborated by Sergeant Avery's account of the slaughter in his undated letter to the governor, where he recounted how one American defender approaching the British to ask for quarter was damned and put to death. He states that "Likewise Colonel Ledyard fair'd his fait in the Same manner."[98]

Physical evidence supports the conclusion that Ledyard was killed by two bayonet thrusts delivered below his armpits along the side seams of his waistcoat. Fortunately, three personal items worn or carried by Ledyard were preserved by his son and daughter-in-law. Those items were Ledyard's sword and his bloodstained waistcoat and shirt containing the killing entry points under the armpits. Those entry points tears are consistent with triangular bayonet thrusts and not with the thrust of the blade of Ledyard's sword.

Ledyard slaying marker in the interior of the fort looking east where the barracks were located.

Seeking Refuge in the Powder Magazine

As the carnage continued, men desperate for safety fled into the powder magazine underneath the southwest bastion and bolted the door. Among them was thirty-five-year-old Lieutenant William Starr, the town's blacksmith, who had come into the fort with two brothers and a cousin. His brother Thomas and his cousin Nicholas were dead. His remaining brother, John, had received a disabling wound to his right arm and lay helpless on the fort's grounds.[99]

Another was nineteen-year-old Joe Moxley, who had entered the fort with his carpenter father, the last man to enter the fort through its north gate. His father had been stabbed in the stomach by a British bayonet and would not live out the night.[100]

Finally, there was sixteen-year-old Stephen Whittlesey who, along with his twenty-three-year-old brother John, had been drafted to serve with the Fort Trumbull garrison. They had escaped across the river with Captain Shapley when that fort was attacked. Now John was dead, shot through the forehead. Young Stephen may have served as a powder monkey and may have found himself trapped in the magazine when the British swarmed into the fort. Unfortunately, the magazine, like the barracks, offered no real protection from the British. A bayonet thrust through an opening in the outer doors would assure that Stephen would join his brother among the martyred.[101]

A platoon of British regulars (probably no more than fifteen men) marched up to where the two outer doors to the magazine made a space wide enough for ten men to stand. At point-blank range, they fired a volley into the magazine, killing and wounding many of the men seeking refuge inside. Lieutenant Starr felt a musket ball hit his breast bone and then travel down his left arm and out his elbow. A musket ball cut through Joe Moxley's waistcoat, ripping it to shreds and grazing his abdomen. He was unhurt, though. It was said that the volley ignited a fire inside the magazine that would have blown up the fort but for the blood of the dead and wounded extinguishing the sparks and flames.[102]

Now another platoon marched up as the platoon that had just volleyed retired. As the new platoon made ready to fire at the magazine, Major Bromfield of the 54th ran up with sword raised and screamed: "Stop firing! You'll send us all to Hell together." This saved the men in the magazine as well as countless British attackers from being blown to pieces in a catastrophic explosion.[103]

Close up of the door to the fort's magazine where some of the fort's defenders sought refuge.

Escaping the Slaughter

Elsewhere, the slaughter continued. Sergeant Hempstead was bayoneted from behind in the hip. Andrew Gallup, who was laid out on the parade ground after being shot, was bayoneted in the arm and was cut deeply across the abdomen by a bayonet thrust that glanced off his ribs. Brothers Andrew and Joshua Baker fought side by side until younger brother Andrew was killed. Joshua too might have been slain when the British soldier aimed his musket butt at his head, but Joshua threw himself backward and the blow fell on his breast bones, breaking all his ribs on one side and effectively taking him down as if he had been slain. He survived but his chest was forever deformed by the want of proper medical care.[104]

As soon as certain defenders realized no quarter was being given, a number fell down among the dead and wounded and feigned death. John Prentiss from Fort Trumbull lay still while the British removed his silver shoe and knee buckles and cut up his hat. He continued to lie among the dead and dying until the British left the fort that evening. Then he crawled out and did what he could to supply water to the dying. Dr. Elisha Morgan also dropped down among the dead and allowed himself to be prodded and robbed. Twenty-one-year old Samuel Edgecomb, who had been hurling eighteen-pound cannon balls at his attackers, saw what was happening on the western and northern side of the fort. Seeing resistance was futile and with his hand wounded, he dropped among the dead and wounded and lay still until the danger had passed. Benajah Holdridge also counterfeited being dead. He was later taken up by the British with the wounded and would later be loaded on to the ill-fated ammunition wagon with other American wounded.[105]

Others, probably on the western wall, jumped from the fort and ran. Among these were Japhet Mason, Stephen Hempstead's brother in law. Henry Mason was another. He was slightly wounded in the leg as he ran from the fort. Despite being wounded in the leg nineteen-year-old Joshua Bill leapt to freedom from the fort's walls. Cary Leeds was less fortunate being on the eastern or northern wall. He had to leap between a gap between the stakes of the fraise and then clear the ditch. This he did but was severely wounded, probably in the process of the jump or by the soldiers firing at him. Samuel Jacques had to kill an attacker before he could jump over the wall and escape unharmed. Still another was Joe Moxley. He had survived the volley fired into the magazine, and after surrendering, managed to jump off the wall and escape in the confusion of the aftermath.[106]

The Northern and Eastern Walls

Little of what has been written concerns the fortunes of those manning the northern and eastern sides of the fort. Captain Burrows, who had poignantly said goodbye to his wife, was killed there by a musket shot to his head. The Chester brothers appear to have been stationed there. Twenty-four-year-old Charles Chester, who was accompanied into the fort by his brothers Ensign Eldredge Chester and Daniel, witnessed their being bayoneted after they surrendered. Unlike his brothers, he did not let go of his musket but remained at the parapet and reloaded it. He then drew back while a British soldier advanced against him. He claims to have leapt onto the barracks which borders the eastern wall. Either he was on the roof or on a second-floor balcony. The soldier pursuing Charles attempted to shoot him, but his musket misfired. His flint probably failed to throw a spark into the pan, a frequent occurrence with any flintlock especially if it had been fired many times and the flint was worn as a result. Charles responded by firing back, but his musket gave him no such trouble but discharged its ball and buckshot into the unlucky Brit. Seeing this from below, a British officer called up to Charles and asked if he did not intend to surrender. To which Charles retorted "Yes, if I can be protected, but not without." The officer responded by promising that he would be protected if he came down from the barracks. Charles could see that the officer had some prisoners gathered around him. He was obviously protecting them, so Charles climbed down and gave himself up.[107]

The Massacre Ends

Fifty-five-year-old Ensign Charles Eldredge, who had sought shelter in the magazine, was badly wounded in knee but bought off a would-be killer by giving the soldier his gold watch. His brother Daniel was spared and would be carried off a prisoner. Edward Stanton was shot in the left breast, which exposed his heart to view. As he lay wounded, he called out to a passing British officer said to be Lieutenant Buskirk of the loyalist 3rd New Jersey and son of its colonel. He begged the lieutenant for something to stanch the flow of blood. The officer offered up his knitted linen nightcap from his pocket as well as water. That small act of kindness saved Stanton's life.[108]

John Daboll, who was wounded in the hand while waging a seven-shot unsuccessful duel with a British soldier before the fort was stormed, was knocked down by the butt of a musket. John begged for his life while the soldier threatened to run him through with his bayonet. A British officer, hearing his pleas, stepped forwarded and knocked the musket away from Daboll's body and declared: "There, you damned rebel, I have saved your life!" Daboll would be paroled to return to his wife.[109]

Major Bromfield of the 54th ordered one of the green- or buff-coated drummers to beat the cease fire. Drummers functioned in the manner of the radiomen of the twentieth century. Their drum beats could be heard above the din of battle to convey the commander's orders. They could be easily spotted by the officers among the hundreds of similarly clothed men since their coats were the facing color of their regiment. Their green (the 54th) or buff coats (40th) were faced with red and they wore black bearskins (the 54th) or white goatskin head-wear (the 40th). By this and other means, the Crown officers slowly gained control over their rampaging men and stopped the slaughter, but not until over half the garrison was dead (eighty-eight) and another quarter wounded, some mortally (forty-one) based on an estimated 155–165 in the fort. The British had suffered close to two hundred killed and wounded (fifty-six killed and 139 wounded) which amounted to more than one quarter of the attackers, estimated to number at least 750.[110]

The British gathered up their own wounded and put them in a part of the fort sheltered from the sun. In contrast, the rebels were ordered to move themselves and their wounded to the shadeless northeast part of the fort. Able-bodied American prisoners were ordered to remove the doors from the barracks and use them as litters to bear the incapacitated British wounded to the shaded part of the fort's parade ground. Then the Americans were told to sit on pain of death and were forbidden from fetching water for their suffering wounded from the fort's well just eleven yards away. Sergeant Avery was successful in persuading the British to give him some water for the wounded and dying.[111]

By late afternoon, the British were getting ready to leave. They marched their prisoners down the steep hill to the riverbank so that they might be embarked for transit to one of the most hellish places on earth at the time, the British prison ships and the Sugar House in New York City. The American wounded who could not move themselves were loaded onto a heavy ammunition wagon on the brow of the hill near the fort's entrance so that they might be brought down the hill to be also shipped to prison, where they most assuredly would die. As the prisoners were removed, the British buried their dead beneath the fort's ravelin. The munitions and ordinance were inventoried. Finally, preparations were made to blow up the fort and all that the Brits could not take with them.

The American dead were left where they were. Among those dead lay Dr. Elisha Morgan, who, though very much alive, remained still to avoid detection. He overheard the British planning for the fort's destruction and waited for an opportunity to frustrate their aim.[112]

Outside the fort, the British attached chains to the ammunition wagon filled with eight severely wounded Americans and thereafter began lowering the wagon down the steep incline from the fort. The weight of the wagon was too much for the weak chain and it snapped. The wagon barreled two hundred feet down the hill with its helpless passengers on a collision course with a large tree stump. On impact, some of these seriously wounded prisoners were thrown from the wagon. Noncombatant Ebenezer Ledyard, a brother of the dead Colonel Ledyard, approached the British about paroling the wounded and offering himself up as hostage. He asked that the seriously wounded Americans be taken into Ensign Ebenezer Avery's home at the foot of the hill. This they did, but the wounded were left to fend for themselves all night while the British looted and set fire to the homes and stores in Groton. Some British soldiers even set fire to the Avery house and Ebenezer Ledyard had to get assistance to put out the flames. He then requested that a British sentry be posted to prevent a reoccurrence of that incident. The

Avery House survived the night and remains today, where it is preserved and maintained by the state.[113]

That evening the British embarked their American prisoners on a ship bound for New York's hellish prison system, where their odds of survival were remote. Most were kept on their respective ships without food or drink for days. Only Washington's decisive victory at Yorktown five weeks later saved most of these men from almost certain death by starvation or disease. Emaciated, they would be released from captivity after three months. Their release was occasioned by Cornwallis' surrender which created an immediate opportunity for prisoners exchanges. Some never recovered from the ill treatment accorded them. Daniel Eldredge returned home on December 3, 1781. The doctor ordered that he partake of cider and suppawn by the spoonful. Instead he took the bowl and drained it. It was too much for his system and he died on December 11.[114]

One final act of British kindness besides the paroling of the wounded was the release of one very lucky twelve-year-old boy, William Latham Jr., son of the fort's captain. The boy asked a British officer what he intended on doing with him. To which the officer replied: "Let you run home to your mother, sonny, if you'll promise not to grow up a damned rebel." Young William wasted no time in so promising.[115]

Around 11 PM, the British lit the slow match fuse to set off the magazine and destroy the fort, and then they embarked on their ships with their spoils, prisoners, and the one hostage and set sail for New York.

Retrieving the Dead and Treating the Wounded

As soon as the British left, Colonel Peters from Norwich entered the fort to search for survivors. He probably ran into Dr. Elisha Morgan, who was similarly waiting for the British to depart to get out from under the pile of dead among whom he had lain for many hours to avoid detection. Morgan probably informed him of the British plans to blow up the fort by detonating the gunpowder in the magazine, located under the southwest bastion. Peters sought out the lit slow match and extinguished it. The fort would remain largely intact to serve as an American base for another 125 years.[116]

The families of the dead and wounded waited for word but feared to approach the fort before they knew that the British had departed. As soon as morning came, members of the families of the garrison and volunteers rushed to the fort to look for their loved ones. One of the first to arrive was the niece of Colonel William Ledyard, Miss Fanny Ledyard. She arrived first and sought out her uncle. Upon finding his corpse, she went to look for the wounded and arrived around 6 AM at the Avery House. There, she tended the wounded by providing them with hot chocolate. When Mrs. Hempstead arrived at the Avery House, she did not recognize her husband and went to the fort to search for him among the dead.[117]

John Burrows entered the fort to seek out his father. He had to turn over twenty-seven bodies before he found the body of his father, killed by a shot to the forehead. Mrs. Chapman sent her three sons to learn the fate of their father, who had been second-in-command at Fort Trumbull. They turned over many bodies, but the majority were so deformed, swollen, and bloodied by their wounds and by being out in the hot sun they could not be sure which body was their father's. Their mother told them if they could not identify their father, then they should pull off the stockings from the feet of the bodies and check for a missing toe. It was only when they found the body with the missing toe that they knew they had found their father.[118]

Many of those who survived suffered horrendous painful and crippling wounds. A report of the special committee appointed in October, 1782, to report to the state's general assembly regarding the requests for aid to these seriously wounded men was delivered on January 2. That report found the following:

Volunteer Captain Charles Eldredge of the militia was hit in the joint of the knee by musket ball and although the wound was closed up, it continued to ooze puss from the broken pieces on bone still lodged in the knee. The knee remained stiff and the limb weak. The prognosis was that it was likely not to improve.

Volunteer John Morgan was also wounded by a musket ball to the knee, which remained stiff and similarly crippling to the man.

Volunteer John Starr received a musket ball through the joint of his right elbow that resulted in the loss of his arm and gave him great pain by reason of the splinters of bone remaining in his arm and the resulting ulcers and oozing sores.

Volunteer Ensign Joseph Woodmansee suffered from a musket ball that took out his right eye and upper part of right cheek and then proceeded to pass through his shoulder blade, seriously weakening it.

Volunteer Captain Solomon Perkins was struck by two musket balls, one through his neck and arm and another through his side. In addition, he received several bayonet thrusts through his stomach that caused him to spasm repeatedly. Understandably, he was determined to be unable to work.

Andrew Gallup, a member of the Griswold's garrison, was shot through the hip and groin, thereby damaging the thigh tendon and preventing him from walking.

Volunteer Lieutenant Parke Avery had part of his cranium removed by a bayonet thrust that also took his right eye.

Volunteer Sergeant Daniel Eldredge was hit by a musket ball that entered his arm somewhere between his wrist and elbow and moved parallel to bone to exit from his upper arm.

Garrison member Zibe Woodworth's thigh bone was fractured and splintered by musket ball. Pieces of the bone protruded from the skin. It left him with a shortened leg and running sores. The committee concluded he would be crippled for life and unable to work.

Trumbull garrison member Sergeant Stephen Hempstead was wounded by a musket shot through the joint of the left elbow and a bayonet thrust through his right hip. Neither wound completely healed. His painful hip wound prevented him from traveling and his elbow wound stiffened and prevented him from lifting his hand to his head.[119]

This is only a partial compilation of the list, but the description brings home the unending lingering effects of wounds that, without being treated with modern medicine, never properly healed and made the lives of those who survived the near massacre a painful existence.

The Post-Battle Reckoning

Arnold returned to New York, where his reception was mixed. He was praised for wiping out a nest of pirates but widely criticized for having lost so many men of the 54th and 40th regiments in his assault on Fort Griswold. This was it for Arnold. He would never again be trusted to lead men into battle. For his countrymen, he would forever be linked with treachery and betrayal in connection with his attempt to surrender West Point, but for his former neighbors of southeastern Connecticut, it would be coupled with a searing hatred borne of the post-surrender slaughter of so many of their loved ones at Fort Griswold.

Nothing would ever be the same again for the citizens of the small town of Groton. There was hardly a family that was not touched by the attack. Besides the loss of so many of their family members and friends, there was the widespread destruction of their homes and property. In New London, 143 buildings were destroyed and ninety-seven families made homeless. In the smaller town of Groton, nineteen buildings were destroyed, including twelve homes and the schoolhouse.[120] It would take years for the towns to recover.

On August 20, 1782 a general court martial was convened in New London and Groton by the Captain General of the state with Brigadier General Roger Newberry presiding. Eight officers and one individual were brought up on charges. Each of the three Connecticut regiments had officers charged, namely the 3rd regiment out of New London, the 20th out of Norwich, the major river port to the north of New London, and the 8th regiment made up of men on the east side of Thames River from the towns of Groton, Stonington and Prescott. The 3rd regiment, the New London unit charged with protecting the city, had the following officers charged with the following results:[121]

1. Lieutenant Colonel Harris was second-in-command of Connecticut's 3rd militia regiment, made up from men in New London and charged primarily with its defense. It was his lack of leadership and cowardly withdrawal from the militia gathered on the invasion route as so described by Jonathan Brooks and John Hempsted. He was charged with being "shamefully negligent" and with cowardice in his failure to carry out the following duties:

   a. To notify his colonel (his immediate superior) of the enemy's approach.

   b. To oppose the enemy's entry into New London.

   c. To support his regiment in the battle to the north of the town after being requested to do so.

   d. To attack the enemy when it was most vulnerable in its retreat from New London.

    e. To establish and maintain control over the militia by allowing them to "remain strolling and unembodied" on a hill in sight of the enemy.

He was found guilty of all five charges and cashiered.

2. Harris's superior, Colonel Jonathan Latimer of the 3rd Connecticut State Regiment, was charged with failing to lead his men forward to prevent the enemy from sacking and burning New London. The reader may remember Brooks's description the militia milling around to the north of town while it burned. Unlike Harris, Latimer was acquitted.

3. Daniel Latimer, ensign of the 3rd regiment, was acquitted of the charge of failing to "seasonably forward intelligence" to his colonel, Jonathan Latimer, undoubtedly a relative. In the eighteenth century, an ensign was the most junior commissioned officer of a regiment. The usually very young junior officer was tasked with carrying the regimental flag in battle. Each battalion would have one or two such officers depending on how many flags the unit had. In the British army, every regiment had two flags: the king's colors and the regimental colors, which were unique to each regiment. In the American army, there was no firm rule. The national colors of the United States were never carried into battle and the number of flags borne by ensigns in American units varied. The position of ensign disappeared in the nineteenth century as the duty of carrying the unit's flags devolved onto noncommissioned officers (sergeants).

The 20th Connecticut State Regiment was made up of men from the Thames River port of Norwich to the north of New London, Arnold's hometown. The regiment had two officers charged in the court martial. Being further away, these men arrived on the hills to the north of New London after the British occupied the town. Jonathan Brooks refers to running into the Norwich militia to the north of New London when they tried to stop him from returning into town. Both men were acquitted.

The colonel of the 20th regiment, Zabdiel Rogers, esquire, was acquitted of the charge of "inactivity."

Major Benajah Leffingwell of the 20th was acquitted of the charge "neglect of duty."

In sharp contrast, the charges levied against five officers of the 8th Connecticut State Regiment were based largely on egregious misbehavior, namely looting and plundering. The 8th regiment was made up of men from Groton and neighboring Stonington to the east and Prescott to the north. Captain John Morgan was found guilty of "neglect of duty and unofficer like behavior." However, his sentence and removal from office were suspended until the American War of Independence ended. He must have done something unmentionable because no description of his behavior was given.

Captain Thomas Wheeler and Lieutenant John Williams of the 8th regiment were cashiered after being found guilty of "plundering in a wanton and shameful manner" goods of the people of Groton. The court forbade their holding of any military commission and required them to pay the expenses of their court martial.

Captain Ebenezer Witter was charged with but acquitted of plundering public property from Fort Griswold because he apparently removed a gun and brought it to his home. He was nevertheless required to return the gun to the fort.

One nonofficer, Warham Williams, was found guilty of stealing three guns. His case was remanded to the civil authorities for punishment.

The Impact of the Near Massacre

We know the terrible impact of the Arnold's attack on New London and Groton, but what about its effect on the rest of the country and on the war for independence?

News traveled very slowly in the eighteenth century. Weeks and months would pass before news of a catastrophe would reach most parts of the country. There was no telegraph, no pony express or national postal service to assure speedy and efficient communication of the news. However horrible the story of the massacre and burning of the towns, it was largely blunted and drowned out by the news five weeks later of the surrender of Cornwallis's army at Yorktown and the virtual end of the war. That wondrous and glorious news of the perceived victorious end of the war tended to drive away the sad and depressing thoughts of past events. People were all too anxious to move on to the more pleasant contemplation of peace and the pursuit of happiness without the fear of war.

Sadly, the close proximation in time of the Arnold raid and the surrender at Yorktown quickly dimmed the memory outside the vicinity of New London and Groton of the terrible events of September 6, 1781. I would not be exaggerating if I were to say that the vast majority of Americans and even residents of Connecticut have never heard of Fort Griswold. Were I not a native Nutmegger, I probably would not have known of the battle; however, my father had a three-volume illustrated tricentennial history of Connecticut published in 1935 that acquainted me as a young boy with the bloody assault against Fort Griswold.

The locals never forgot what happened at the fort. Some of the survivors lived to ripe old ages and wrote of their experiences of the battle. At least one of the survivors was alive into the 1850s some seventy or more years after the battle which so marked their lives.

In 1826, some fifty years after the signing of the Declaration of Independence, the citizens of Groton, not wanting posterity to forget their sacrifice of 1781, petitioned the Connecticut General Assembly to charter an organization for the purpose raising funds by a lottery for building a proper memorial to commemorate their citizen heroes of Fort Griswold. They chose to build a monument a few yards away from the fort in the form of a giant obelisk or pyramidon, 135 feet high with an inner spiral stairway composed of 165 steps. The cornerstone was laid on the anniversary date of the battle in 1826. It was designed to sit on a base of twenty-two square feet. The monument was to be constructed of locally cut granite.

The monument was completed in four years and dedicated on September 6, 1830, the first such monument built in the United States. It stood 265 feet above the harbor. The Fort Griswold monument would be followed years later by both the taller Bunker Hill Monument and the Washington Monument.

Restoration and Use of the Fort After 1781

Although the defenders of Forts Griswold and Trumbull brought honor to their communities, the conduct of the militia outside the forts was shameful, especially those engaged in enriching themselves by participating in looting the property of their neighbors in Groton.

There was no question the forts were undermanned and poorly maintained. The people of New London and Groton petitioned the general assembly to restore and properly man the forts, but the American Revolution was coming to a close. Fort Griswold was manned by federal troops during the War of 1812 to protect New London from the threat of a British assault. In May of 1813, Commodore Stephen Decatur commanding the frigate *United States* and the *Macedonian*, a frigate captured from the British and newly refitted as an American warship, sought refuge under the guns of Fort Griswold. A squadron of the Royal Navy was hunting his two ships and chased Decatur into the Thames River. The British blockaded the river for a time, but never made an attempt to go upriver to challenge the American defenses.[122]

After the War of 1812, the fort would continue to live on as a military base into the early twentieth century, when it would at last be turned over to the state of Connecticut for a state park, though with a constant threat of development from those who have forgotten the sacrifice of their forbears.

The Fort and
Monument Today

The fort and the monument are part of the Connecticut state park system. The Fort Griswold Battlefield State Park consists of the remains of the fort, the monument, and the Monument House Museum, which sits on approximately seventeen acres. The museum and monument are open only during the summer, from Memorial Day until Labor Day. The fort is open year-round. It is administered by the Connecticut Department of Energy and Environmental Protection. The fort and water battery below were part of the US Army's seacoast defenses until around 1908, when its use was largely supplanted by Fort H. G. Wright on Fishers Island in Long Island Sound.[123]

Fort Trumbull, on the other hand, was dismantled and rebuilt in the 1830s as a masonry fortification as part of the Third System" of seacoast defenses along the lines of other post War of 1812 fortifications like Fort Pulaski, Fort Point, and Fort Sumter. Fort Griswold did not suffer the same fate, so it appears largely as it was in 1781, but evidencing the wear of almost two and a half centuries of neglect. Its features and outline remain, but its fosses and wall are eroded. The gun platforms, fraise, embrasures, gate and barracks have long since disappeared. The museum, which served as the home for the monument caretaker, has a broad assortment of historic artifacts, many of which are totally unrelated to the Revolution or the battle that took place there. Two original pieces of clothing from the battle are on display: a round hat purportedly worn by one of the defenders and a red shawl worn by Sergeant Avery as he stood watch the evening before the battle.

There is a fairly good diorama showing the assault on the fort. It shows abatis around the fort even though there is no mention of it in the accounts of the battle. The museum contains a large mural painting depicting the aftermath of the battle. It mistakenly features grenadiers of the 54th Regiment and several other inaccuracies.

The museum also contains two uniformed dummies purporting to show the uniform worn by Colonel Ledyard and the other the uniform of a member of the two artillery companies assigned to Fort Trumbull and Fort Griswold. These would appear to conform with General Washington's uniform regulations issued in 1779. These regulations were often honored in the breach. My educated guess is that Colonel Ledyard would not have worn the blue coat faced white because he was not part of a Continental infantry unit, but rather the colonel of two artillery companies that may or may have not been members of the Continental establishment.

Finally, there is the plaque in the fort depicting Ledyard's orderly or servant Jordan Freeman dressed as a southern cotton field slave, barefooted and hatless. I think it to be a particularly thoughtless and insulting portrayal of an African American hero, who was not a slave and who, as the personal servant and representative of the commanding officer of all Connecticut troops east of the Connecticut River, would, if anything, have been finely dressed from head to toe as he represented the very pinnacle of command and society under Colonel William Ledyard.

In the author's humble opinion, the state and the many historical societies in the area should lend a greater hand to preserve and restore this singular site of bravery and sacrifice as well as tragedy and betrayal during the waning days of our fight for independence. For the state of Connecticut, it is the site of its bloodiest day of battle. A few years ago, the monument had deteriorated so much that it was no longer safe to enter. Emergency funds were eventually made available to restore the monument and reopen it to the public.

The fort itself has never been restored. What remains are the walls, the bastions and the sally port, which sit in silent witness to the sacrifice of American patriots of all races and the bloody and tragic event that has been largely forgotten by the American people. I hope this book revives some interest in this long-ago event and restore our memory of the events of a day that helped make America.

I urge the state of Connecticut, my native state, to undertake an archeological study of the fort and its environs, restore the fort to its 1781 appearance, and update its museum collection to accurately tell the story the Alamo of the American Revolution, Fort Griswold.

Commentary on Three Maps

A s mentioned in the prologue, much of my understanding of what occurred on the Arnold expedition against New London and Groton is derived from my careful analysis of three maps generated in the aftermath of the assault on Fort Griswold and the burning of New London. The foremost of these is the hand-drawn sketch of the fort and notes by an ensign of Britain's 40th regiment of foot, Ensign Alexander Gray. The 40th regiment was one of two British regiments of foot that engaged in the assault with the other being the 54th regiment of foot, whose commander Lieutenant Colonel Eyre was in overall command of the all-British force on the east side of the Thames River.

The rank of ensign was the lowest rank of commissioned officer in the infantry beneath the rank of lieutenant. The ensign's responsibility was to carry one of two flags carried by each battalion of a regiment, namely the king's colors or the regimental colors. The position was normally held by the most junior and quite often one of the youngest of the officers' corps. The position largely disappeared in the nineteenth century when the responsibility for carrying a unit's flags devolved onto sergeants, who are noncommissioned officers.

We do not know if the 40th and 54th Regiments brought their flags on the expeditions. There is no mention of them in the accounts I have seen, but it would appear that their ensigns were present and therefore eyewitnesses to the fighting. Because of this, we would expect Gray's map to be the most accurate of the engagement and, to the extent of discrepancies with the other mapmakers, to be more credible.

That being said, Gray's map is simpler and a good deal less detailed than the Faden map. Unlike the Faden map, it does not reveal the location of the fort's embrasures and places only four of the twenty-three cannon supposedly mounted on the fort's parapet shown on the Faden map. Gray's map does not show the location of the flagstaff, the fort's well, the fort's fosse, and the ditch leading from the sally port to the water battery.

Gray appears to have focused only on the approaches of the 40th Regiment and the guns bearing on them so it is not clear if other guns were effectively firing on troops of the 54th regiment. He notes the two 9-pounders located in the eastern flanks of the two bastions "doing a Great Deal of Mischief" by presumably enfilading attackers along the north and south walls. The Faden map identifies only the 9-pounder in the southwest bastion.

Gray marks what I deduced to be the location of Sergeant Hempstead's 18-pounder and its companion gun mentioned by Hempstead in his memoirs located on the opposite side by the fort's gate on the north wall. Gray specifically identifies where the light and grenadier companies of the 40th Regiment in and around the northeast corner of the fort "carried the work." From his notes, it appears that at least some of the battalion companies of the 40th attacked along the south curtain wall and southeast corner. No map clearly delineates where the 54th Regiment concentrated their attacks, but we can surmise there must have been part of that unit on the north wall and the southwest bastion by reason that Gray does not place the 40th's assault on those positions.

The Faden map, by contrast, is a printed map by a known London printer. Unlike Gray's map, it clearly shows each embrasure on the fort's walls and the placement of each gun on the fort's parapets. From the map, we can clearly see there were four empty embrasures on the south wall but only two on the north wall. Three empty embrasures were located in the northeast corner, the exact spot that Gray identifies as the location of the breakthrough by 40th's two flank companies (lights and grenadiers). Attacking through an embrasure not being occupied by the muzzle of a cannon barrel was obviously easier and safer than otherwise.

One can also deduce the approximate size of the cannon placed *en barbette* on the side facing the river and those at the embrasures by comparing the size of the lines representing the barrels. The 12-pounders, 9-pounders, and the one 18-pounder can be identified by longer lines. The very short barrel lines of the cannon on the east wall signify 4- and 6-pounders facing the country, where longer range would count for less. The riverside cannon, in contrast, were intended to cover the almost mile wide-river and heavily armed ships coming up the river.

As an added bonus, the Faden map also shows not only the location of the fort's flagstaff, but also a depiction of the striped flag flying over the southwest bastion. It would appear to be a simple thirteen-striped flag with no corner canton for the thirteen stars. The Betsy Ross-style flag was still not very common on land even in 1781. Different states and localities flew their own version of a national flag. We don't even know if the stripes were white and red, but an educated guess was that they were, and the flag may have contained a popular symbol such as a snake lying diagonally across the thirteen red and white stripes.

The Faden map's major discrepancies with the Gray map are in the placement of the 40th Regiment's flank companies on the south wall. This runs counter to the Gray map, which shows those companies on the northeast corner of the fort. Faden also shows the ditch or fosse as continuing along the south wall. We know from notes on the Gray map and the fort's builders' description that the Faden map is wrong. As stated earlier, I believe Gray's hand-drawn map to be more reliable than the Faden map.

Finally, there is the published hand-drawn map by Captain Daniel Lyman of the Arnold's loyalist American Legion Regiment who had earlier resided in Pomfret, Connecticut. He was a fellow Nutmegger and at one time or another, appears to have befriended Arnold. Lyman's map shows in great detail the entire Arnold expeditionary movements on both New London and its forts as well as the approach to Fort Griswold by Eyre's three regiments and Jägers. It shows the alignment of each unit and the various roads or paths taken.

To that end, I point to the alignment of the 54th and 40th regiments on their assault approaches to Fort Griswold. It clearly shows the 40th regiment to the right of the 54th regiment at the beginning of the assault with the 54th aimed more or less against the south and east walls of the fort and the 40th attacking toward the northeast corner and eastern wall of the fort. It shows the detached flèche lying a hundred or more yards to the east northeast of the fort. The map clearly shows that the 4th battalion, New Jersey Volunteers, and Royal Artillery taking a more circuitous route to the fort and thus arriving after the fort was taken. It also shows the Jägers stationed north of the fort on the road to

Stonington and due east of the fort in a blocking position to any American reinforcements coming from the east.

The map shows each of Arnold's units on the west side of the Thames River and their approaches from the beaches. It shows how Upham's Refugees and the American Legion marched to the west and parallel to Arnold's main column advancing up the principal highway to New London from the beaches on what is now Ocean Avenue. Upham's Refugees and the American Legion are the troops that advanced around the west flank of Fort Nonsense and encountered John Hempsted and his fellow volunteers in the process.

The map is detailed enough to show the cannon abandoned by Hempsted on Manwaring Hill. It also shows the church on the hill to the east of Manwaring Hill, where the one Royal Artillery piece brought by Arnold was placed to fire on the American privateers escaping upriver.

All in all, the three maps taken together provide a wealth of detailed information on the Arnold expedition.

Were the Troops of Forts Griswold and Trumbull Uniformed?

G iven the fact that Connecticut was called the "Provision State" and its continental soldiers so well uniformed that the state turned down the French-made-and-supplied lottery coats given to the soldiers of other states in 1778 and 1779, it is highly likely the two state artillery companies garrisoning Forts Trumbull and Griswold were uniformed. Although Washington's general orders of October 2, 1779, provided that New England troops be uniformed with blue coats faced white, the orders also provided that troops in the artillery be outfitted in blue coats faced and lined in scarlet edged with yellow tape and yellow button holes with yellow buttons and yellow tape-bound cocked hats.[124] Therefore, I believe that the garrisons of the two forts would be uniformed similarly. Alternatively, they might have worn the earlier version of the artilleryman's uniform by men from Connecticut, a black coat with red facings and yellow buttons.

American Casualties and Survivors

These lists of names and other relevant information were compiled by Charles Allyn for his centennial work *Battle of Groton Heights* published in 1882. Mr. Allyn noted that many names were left off the monument or had different spellings of their names. He added and corrected several names.[125]

KILLED

(Name, residence)

Captain Elijah Avery, Groton

Captain Elisha Avery, Groton

Lieutenant Ebenezer Avery, Groton

Ensign Daniel Avery, Groton

Sergeant Christopher Avery, Groton

Sergeant Jasper Avery, Groton

Sergeant Solomon Avery, Groton

David Avery, Groton

Thomas Avery, Groton

Captain Samuel Allyn, Groton (Ledyard)

Captain Simeon Allyn, Groton (Ledyard)

Belton Allyn, Groton (Ledyard)

Benadem Allyn, Groton(Ledyard)

Nathaniel Adams, Groton

Captain Hubbard Burrows, Groton

Sergeant Ezekiel Bailey, Groton

Corp. Andrew Billings, Groton-Ledyard

Andrew Baker, Groton(Ledyard)

John P. Babcock, Groton

John Billings, Preston

Samuel Billings, Groton

William Bolton, New London

John Brown, Groton

Jonathan Butler, Saybrook

Lieut. Richard Chapman, New London

Sergeant Eldredge Chester, Groton

Daniel Chester, Groton

Jedidiah Chester, Groton

Frederic Chester, Groton

John Clark, New London

Elias Coit, New London

Lieut. James Comstock, New London

William Comstock, Saybrook

Philip Covill, Groton

Daniel Davis, Groton

Daniel Eldredge, Groton

Jordan Freeman (Black), Groton

Capt. Elias Henry Halsey, Long Island

Samuel Hill, Groton-Ledyard

John Holt, Jr, New London

Sergeant Rufus Hurlburt, Groton-Ledyard

Eliday Jones, Groton

Moses Jones, Groton-Ledyard

Benoni Kenson, New London

Barney Kinney, New London

Captain Youngs Ledyard, Groton

Lieut. Col. William Ledyard, Groton

Captain Cary Leeds, Groton

Lieut. Joseph Lewis, Groton-Ledyard

Ensign John Lester, .Groton-Ledyard

Daniel D. Lester, ,Groton

Jonas Lester, .Groton

Wait Lester, Groton

Thomas Lamb, Groton

Lambo Latham (Black), Groton

Captain Nathan Moore, .Groton

Corporal Edward Mills, Groton

Corp. Simeon Morgan, Groton-Ledyard

Thomas Miner, Groton-Ledyard

Joseph Moxley, Groton-Ledyard

Corp. Luke Perkins, Jr, Groton-Ledyard

David Palmer, Groton

Elisha Perkins, Groton-Ledyard

Luke Perkins, ,Groton-Ledyard

Asa Perkins, Groton-Ledyard

Elnathan Perkins, Groton-Ledyard

Simeon Perkins, Groton-Ledyard

Captain Peter Richards, .New London

Captain Adam Shapley, .New London

Captain Amos Stanton,, Groton-Ledyard

Lieut. Enoch Stanton, Stonington

Sergeant Daniel Stanton, Stonington

Sergeant John Stedman, Groton-Ledyard

Sergeant Nicholas Starr, Groton

Corporal Nathan Sholes, .Groton-Ledyard

Thomas Starr, Jr, Groton

David Seabury, Groton-Ledyard

Captain John Williams, ,Groton

Lieut. Henry Williams, Groton-Ledyards

Lieut. Patric Ward, Groton

Sylvester Walworth, Groton

Joseph Wedger, Groton-Ledyard

Thomas Williams, ,Stonington

Daniel Williams, Saybrook

John Whittlesey, Saybrook

Stephen Whittlesey, Saybrook

Christopher Woodbridge, Groton

Henry Woodbridge, Groton

CAPTURED

(Name, wound, residence)

Lieut. Parke Avery, Jr., lost eye, Groton

Ensign Ebenezer Avery, head, Groton

Amos Avery, hand wound, Groton

John Daboll, Jr., hand wound, Groton

Ensign Charles Eldredge, knee, Groton

Daniel Eldredge, shot neck & face, Groton

Christopher Eldredge, face, Groton

Samuel Edgecomb, Jr., hand, Groton

Andrew Gallup, hip, Groton

Robert Gallup, in the body, Groton

Sgt. S. Hempstead, body, New London

Corporal Jehial Judd, knee, Hebron

Captain William Latham, thigh, .Groton

Captain Edward Latham, body, Groton

Jonathan Latham, Jr., body, Groton

Christopher Latham, Jr., body, Groton

Frederic Moore, body, Groton

John Morgan, knee, Groton

Jabish Pendleton, hand, Groton

Captain Solomon Perkins, face, Groton

Lieut. Obadiah Perkins, breast, Groton

Ebenezer Perkins, face. Groton

Elisha Prior, arm, .Groton

Lieut. William Starr, breast, Groton

John Starr, arm, Groton

Daniel Stanton, Jr., body, Stonington

Edward Stanton, body, Stonington

Samuel Stillman, arm & thigh, Saybrook

William Seymour, leg lost, Hartford

Tom Wansac, (Pequot) neck, Groton

Ensign Joseph Woodmansee, one eye, Groton

Sanford Williams, body, Groton

Asel Woodworth, leg, Groton

Thomas Woodworth, leg, Groton

Zibe Woodworth, knee, Groton

These wounded defenders were paroled by Major Bromfield, the commanding officer of British forces on the east bank of Thames River. That was an act of mercy, for certainly none would have survived given the exiguous treatment of American prisoners in the notorious New York Sugar House.

CAPTURED DEFENDERS, TAKEN TO THE SUGAR HOUSE

Sergeant Rufus Avery

Peter Avery

Caleb Avery

Samuel Abraham

Joshua Baker

Reuben Bushnell

Captain William Coit (taken in New London)

Charles Chester

Nathan Darrow

Elias Dart

Levi Dart

Gilbert Eldredge

Ebenezer Fish

Walter Harris

Jeremiah Harding

Mr. Kilburn

Ebenezer Ledyard (hostage)

William Latham

Jonathan Minor

Isaac Morgan

Isaac Rowley

Lieut. Jabez Stow of Saybrook captured at Fort Trumbull

Corporal Josiah Smith

Holsey Sanford

Solomon Tift

Horatio Wales

Thomas Welles

The prisoners suffered from the want of food and water almost from the start. But for the victory at Yorktown on October 19, many of those captured from the attack on Groton and New London would have perished from severe deprivation.

The prisoners appear to have been released in early December. Daniel Eldredge returned home on December 3, 1781. He was sick, starved, and nearly dead. His doctor advised him to eat small portions to regain his health. Despite that advice, Daniel consumed an entire bowl of cider and suppawn on or about December 11, resulting in almost instant death.[126]

ESCAPEES AMONG THE DEFENDERS

The following individuals, seeing that the British were not accepting the surrender of any of the defenders, sought refuge by leaping over the parapets. The problems with making any attempt to escape were clearing the pickets or fraise and landing in the ditch below without injury, all the while being fired upon by the British. It should be no surprise that the many suffered injuries in the process. Only if they could leap off the western wall, where there was no fraise and no ditch, could they be more assured of a safe landing.

The following individuals successfully leaped off the fort's parapets:

Benjamin Bill, ankle wound, Groton

Joshua Bill, leg injury, Groton

Benajah Holdridge, feigned death before leaping, Groton

Samuel W. Jaques, Exeter, R.I.

Amos Lester, hip injury, Groton

Cary Leeds, escaped but died of his wounds, Groton

Henry Mason, leg injury, Groton

James Morgan, 15 bayonet pricks on his back and legs, Groton

Thomas Mallison, fought hand to hand and leaped over parapet and fraising, Groton

Note that wounds suffered by many of the aforementioned escapees are the injuries they sustained in leaping from the fort's parapets.

The following individuals escaped capture by feigning death by lying underneath the bodies of their colleagues:

Elisha Morgan, Groton

John Prentis, New London

The following individuals also escaped capture for other reasons:

William Latham Jr.: the twelve-year-old son of the fort's commander, released by the British because of his age.

Japhet Mason of Groton: no story about how he avoided capture.

Elijah Bailey: avoided capture after firing the guns in the northeast flèche at the beginning of the assault by running down the hill on the west side of the fort and hiding in a cornfield.

There is much that may be surmised by the lists. You may note the number of family that fought and died or were wounded in the engagement. For example, Elnathan Perkins went into the fort with his four sons and all perished but one son and he was wounded. Two other Perkinses were wounded. The losses were devastating to a small community where families were so close and interrelated.

Those on the list from Groton or Ledyard, which was part of Groton at the time, were part of the garrisons or the militia. Those listed as coming from towns west of the Thames River such as Saybrook or New London were probably from the Fort Trumbull garrison or one of the privateers. Those from towns further east or north of Groton, such as Stonington, Hartford or Exeter, Rhode Island, may have been visiting someone or been a member of the privateer crews.

Acknowledgments

No man is an island, and no nonfiction author is separate and apart from his predecessors who tackled the subject before him—and the many experts on technical aspects of eighteenth century. I want to single out for special assistance and expert advice on eighteenth-century fortifications and artillery Dr. Glenn Williams, a noted author on the American frontier during the period of the Revolution and an official US Army historian and officer. He provided invaluable information on Revolutionary War fortifications and artillery and the proper terminology regarding the same. I also want to thank fellow author and historian Larry Kidder, who has assisted me by creating detailed maps of the fort. I also wish to thank my son Asher Lurie of the Old Barracks Museum in Trenton for advice on uniforms and illustrations. Finally, I wish to thank Roger Williams, who shepherded this book for publication.

Bibliography

Caulkins, Frances Manwaring. *History of New London, Connecticut*. Case, Lockwood and Company, 1860.

Chartrand, Rene. *Forts of the American Revolution 1775-83*. Oxford, U.K.: Osprey Publishing Ltd., 2016.

———. *Ticonderoga 1758 Montcalm's Victory Against all Odds*. Oxford, U.K.: Osprey Publishing Ltd., 2000.

Clement, Justin. *Philadelphia 1777: Taking the Capital*. Oxford, U.K.: Osprey Publishing Ltd., 2007.

Fleming, Thomas J. *Now We Are Enemies*. New York: St. Martin's Press, 1960.

Galvin, Major John R. *The Minute Men*. New York: Hawthorn Books, Inc., 1967.

Hall, Bert S. *Weapons and Warfare in Renaissance Europe*. Baltimore, MD: The John Hopkins University Press, 1997.

Harris, William W. *The Battle of Groton Heights: A Collection of Narratives, Official Reports, Records etc. of the Storming of Fort Griswold, the Massacre of its Garrison, and the Burning of New London by British Troops under the Command of Brig. Gen. Benedict Arnold, on the Sixth of Sept., 1781.* New London, CT: Charles Allyn, 1882.

Katcher, Philip. *Uniforms of the Continental Army,* York, PA: George Shumway Publisher, 1981.

Lefferts, Lieutenant Charles M. *Uniforms of the American, British, French and German Armies of the American Revolution.* New York: WE Inc., 1927.

Lehman, Eric D. *Homegrown Terror: Benedict Arnold and the Burning of New London.* Middletown, CT: Wesleyan University Press, 2014.

Lossing, Benson J., *The Pictorial Field-Book of the Revolution.* Rutland, Vermont: Charles E. Tuttle Company, 1859.

Mancini, Jason R. and David J. Naumec. *Connecticut's African & Native American Revolutionary War Enlistments 1775-1783.* The Mashantucket Pequot Museum & Research Center, 2005.

Martin, James Kirby. *Benedict Arnold: Revolutionary Hero.* New York: New York University Press, 1997.

Nevin, David. *The Texans.* Alexandria, VA: Time-Life Books, 1982.

Novak, Greg. *The American War of Independence—A Guide to the Armies of the American War of Independence, Book 1: The Northern Campaigns,* Old Glory Corp.

Powell, Dr. Walter L. *Murder or Mayhem? Benedict Arnold's New London, Connecticut Raid, 1781.* Gettysburg, PA: Thomas Publications, 2000.

Randall, Willard Sterne. *Benedict Arnold Patriot and Traitor.* New York: William Morrow and Company, Inc., 1990.

Reid, Stuart. *The Battle of Minden 1759: The Impossible Victory of the Seven Years War*. Frontline Books, 2016.

Smith, Carolyn and Helen Vergason. *September 6, 1781: North Groton's Story*. New London, CT: New London Printers, 1981.

Spring, Matthew H., *With Zeal and with Bayonets Only*. Norman, OK: University of Oklahoma Press, 2008.

Troiani, Don. "Fort Griswold." American Heritage, October, 1973, Volume XXIV, Number 6.

White, David O., *Connecticut's Black Soldiers 1775-1783*. Chester, CT: Pequot Press, 1973.

Endnotes

1   Harris, William W. *The Battle of Groton Heights: A Collection of Narratives, Official Reports, Records etc. of the Storming of Fort Griswold, the Massacre of its Garrison, and the Burning of New London by British Troops under the Command of Brig. Gen. Benedict Arnold, on the Sixth of Sept., 1781.* Rev Charles Allyn. New London, CT: Charles Allyn, 1882, 266-273.

2   Novak, Greg. *The American War of Independence-A Guide to the Armies of the American War of Independence, Book One, the Northern Campaigns,* Old Glory Corp., 127

3   Lossing, Benson J., *The Pictorial Field-Book of the Revolution,* Charles E. Tuttle Company, Rutland, Vermont, 1859. 609.

4   Harris, *Groton Heights,* 241-242.

5   Ibid. 241.

6   Ibid. 270.

7   Lehman, Eric D, *Homegrown Terror,* Wesleyan University Press, Middletown, Connecticut, 151n

8   Ibid. 100.

9   Powell, Dr. Walter L. *Murder or Mayhem? Benedict Arnold's New London, Connecticut Raid, 1781.* Gettysburg, PA. Thomas Publications, 2000, 13-23.

10 Ibid. 10.

11 See William Faden Map of Fort Griswold

12 Chartrand, Rene. *Forts of the American Revolution 1775-83.* Osprey Publishing Ltd. Oxford, U.K. 2016, 61-63.

13   See William Faden Map of Fort Griswold

14   Ibid.

15   Powell, *Murder or Mayhem?*, 18

16   Ibid. 14.

17   Troiani, Don. *Fort Griswold*. American Heritage, October, 1973, Volume XXIV, Number 6, 69-70

18   Smith, Carolyn & Helen Vergason. *September 6, 1781: North Groton's Story*. New London, CT: New London Printers, 1981

19   Ibid.

20   Powell, *Murder or Mayhem?*, 8-9

21   Ibid. 24-29

22   Lefferts, Lt. Charles. *Uniforms of the American, British, French and German Armies of the American Revolution*. New York, 1927. 229

23   Novak, *The American War of Independence Book One*, 127

24   Powell, *Murder or Mayhem?*, 32

25   Harris, *Groton Heights,* 30

26   Powell, *Murder or Mayhem?*, 27

27   Ibid. 33

28   Harris, *Groton Heights,* 232 & 260

29   Caulkins, Frances Manwaring. *History of New London, Connecticut*. Case, Lockwood and Company, 1860. Chapter XXXII, Part Two, 545-572.

30   Harris, *Groton Heights,* 259-260

31   Ibid. 238-239

32   Ibid. 50-51

33   Ibid. 236

34   Ibid. 261-265

35   Ibid. 241

36   Ibid. 224-225

37   Novak, *The American War of Independence Book One*, 127

38   Harris, *Groton Heights,* 62

39   Ibid. 64

40   Ibid. 76

41   Ibid. 77

42   Ibid. 63

43   Ibid. 65

44   Ibid.

45   Ibid. 67

46   Ibid. 77-82

47   Ibid. 78
48   Ibid. 99
49   Ibid.
50   Ibid. 48
51   Ibid. 229
52   Ibid. 102
53   Ibid. 100
54   Caulkins, *History of New London*. 545-572
55   Ibid.
56   Powell, *Murder or Mayhem?*, 39
57   Caulkins, *History of New London*. 545-572, Part 2
58   Ibid.
59   Lehman, *Homegrown Terror*, 148
60   Ibid. 146.
61   Powell, *Murder or Mayhem?*, 42
62   Caulkins, *History of New London*. 545-572, Part 2
63   Ibid.
64   Lehman, *Homegrown Terror*, 149
65   Powell, *Murder or Mayhem?*,60
66   Harris, *Groton Heights*, 262
67   See Lyman's map.
68   Powell, *Murder or Mayhem?*, 43
69   Harris, *Groton Heights*, 32
70   Ibid. 65
71   Ibid. 87
72   Powell, *Murder or Mayhem?*, 46
73   Harris, *Groton Heights*. 106-107
74   Ibid. 33
75   Ibid.234
76   Ibid.
77   Ibid.212-265
78   Ibid. 33
79   Hall, Bert S., *Weapons and Warfare in Renaissance Europe*. Baltimore, MD. The John Hopkins University Press. 1997. 134-156
80   Harris, *Groton Heights*. 106
81   Ibid. 248
82   Ibid. 49
83   Powell, *Murder or Mayhem?*, 78
84   See Ensign Gray's Map

85   Harris, *Groton Heights.* 231
86   Ibid. 51
87   Ibid. 33
88   Ibid. 50
89   Ibid. 51
90   Ibid. 238
91   Ibid. 224
92   Ibid. 241
93   Ibid. 251
94   Ibid. 34
95   Ibid. 29-44
96   Ibid. 52
97   Powell, *Murder or Mayhem?,* 60-66
98   Harris, *Groton Heights.* 64
99   Ibid. 226
100   Ibid. 241
101   Ibid. 260-261
102   Ibid. 241
103   Ibid. 38
104   Ibid. 228
105   Ibid. 212-265
106   Ibid.
107   Ibid. 237-240
108   Ibid. 264
109   Ibid. 231
110   Lossing, *The Pictorial Field-Book of the Revolution,* 612
111   Ibid. 39
112   Ibid. 247-248n
113   Ibid. 257
114   Ibid. 243
115   Ibid. 227
116   Ibid. 247
117   Ibid. 54-55
118   Ibid. 230
119   Ibid. 128-131
120   Ibid. 27-28
121   Ibid. 113-117
122   Lossing, *The Pictorial Field-Book of the Revolution,* 613

ENDNOTES

123   History of Fort Griswold brochure, Fort Griswold Park Foundation

124   Katcher, Philip. *Uniforms of the Continental Army,* York, PA., George Shumway Publisher, 1981, 27.

125   Harris, *Groton Heights,* 266-272

126   Ibid. 243.

About the Author

Jerry Hurwitz is a native of the state of Connecticut, where as a young child he first learned about the bloody assault on Fort Griswold from a tricentennial illustrated history of the state published in 1935. This led to a lifelong passion for learning about the American Revolution. Hurwitz is a graduate of Lehigh University and the University of Connecticut Law School and has been a practicing attorney for forty-five years. He has served as president of the Princeton Battlefield Society for twenty years, a nonprofit corporation dedicated to preserving and restoring the Princeton Battlefield. As president, he engaged in a thirteen-year struggle to save a core area of the battlefield from a housing development. He has lectured about and given tours of the Princeton Battlefield. He has also written magazine articles on the Battle of Princeton and on the massacre of Fort Griswold. Hurwitz has been a longstanding member of the Company of Military Historians, the American Battlefield Trust, and the 43rd Regiment of Foot/2nd Pennsylvania Regiment. He currently resides and works near Tampa, Florida.